From Your Coffee Shop Dream, To Your Dream Coffee Shop

SAMUEL GUREL

ALEXANDRA MOSHER

SCI Press
Portland, Oregon
2021

Copyright © 2021 Sustainable Coffee Institute

All rights reserved. No part of this publication may be reproduced, distributed, or transmitted in any form or by any means, including photocopying, recording, or other electronic or mechanical methods, without the prior written permission of the publisher, except in the case of brief quotations embodied in critical reviews and certain other noncommercial uses permitted by copyright law. For permission requests, write to the publisher, addressed "Attention: Permissions Coordinator," at the address below.

ISBN: 9781736885925 (Hardcover)
ISBN: 9781736885918 (Ebook)

Any references to historical events, real people, or real places are used fictitiously. Names, characters, and places are products of the author's imagination.

Front cover image by Davis Butler.

Printed by Ingram Spark in the United States of America.

First printing edition 2021.

Sustainable Coffee Institute
2336 N Randolph Ave.
Portland, OR 97227

www.sci.coffee

Contents

Introduction — 5

Part I The Problem
Chapter 1: The Beginning — 7
Chapter 2: The Meeting — 15
Chapter 3: Getting Started — 22

Part II Gaining Clarity
Chapter 4: Vulnerability — 30
Chapter 5: Culture — 38
Chapter 6: Strategy — 47
Chapter 7: Tactics — 57
Chapter 8: Introduction to Systems — 62

Part III Systems
Chapter 9: Finances — 73
Chapter 10: Hiring — 79
Chapter 11: Customer Service — 86
Chapter 12: Inventory — 91
Chapter 13: Decision Making — 94

Part IV Communicating Culture
Chapter 14: Foundational Culture — 102
Chapter 15: Strategic Culture — 107
Chapter 16: Team Communication — 112
Chapter 17: Marketing Alignment — 116
Chapter 18: The End — 119

Introduction

The Sustainable Coffee Institute is so convinced that the most important step business owners can take for the success of their business is to understand their culture intimately. So, when we set out to write a book, we were unsure about how to best convey this idea. Eventually, we landed on the idea of a "business fable" and here's why: it allows you to learn through a storyline rather than the traditional, "How To" book. Coffee people aren't reading traditional business books (which may be a part of the problem) so we decided to do something different. We've been heavily influenced by Patrick Lencioni and his ideas concerning business culture. Some of the concepts in this book have been adapted and added from Patrick's amazing work.

So why are we doing this?

The Sustainable Coffee Institute is committed to both environmental sustainability and financial sustainability. We are committed and invested in business education, specifically geared toward the coffee industry and this book is a part of that work.

The world of Claire Wallace is fictional, but SCI is thankful to all the very real coffee shop owners who vulnerably shared their journey with us. They did so to show you that you're not alone and that there is hope. Lots of it.

Part I
The Problem

Chapter 1: The Beginning

It was the perfect day to be in a coffee shop. Summer had just walked out the door and fall was making her entrance. After months of blistering heat, the cool, gentle rain was welcome.

Claire Wallace cradled her latte in her hands and brought it up to her lips, stopping for a moment to inhale the sweet smell of cinnamon.

Nothing could please her more than this moment; tucked away in a warm café, drinking a fall-themed latte that wasn't too syrupy or too bitter. This was exactly what she needed after a week in her mundane, corporate-America job.

There was a time when she had sworn that she would never work a boring job. She'd done pretty well, too, traveling around South America, taking odd jobs, picking up freelance work, sometimes waitressing to survive.

And then somewhere along the way, she got tired. At the age of twenty-six, she desired a well-paying job that offered security and stability.

She'd enjoyed the first year. The second year was a little less fun. But by the third year it felt like her soul was being sucked out with a straw.

Wasn't there more to life than stability and security? And yet, at the age of twenty-nine, she was also beginning to dream about meeting the right man and starting a family. Her prince could walk through the door any day now!

The bell on the door of the coffee shop rang as someone walked inside.

Claire turned around, half-expecting to lock eyes with her long-awaited lover, only to see her longtime friend, Maggie Reynolds.

Her face fell.

"Don't look so excited to see me." Maggie playfully smacked Claire's arm then plopped down next to her, unraveling the scarf around her neck.

"Sorry, I thought you were going to be the man of my dreams," Claire admitted with a smile.

Maggie let out a bright laugh. "You're such a nerd, Claire."

"Try this." Claire slid her drink over to Maggie. "I was just imagining my way out of corporate America."

Maggie brought the drink to her lips and her eyes lit up. "Mmm, yummy. Is fall really here already?" She set the drink back down in front of Claire. "So, have you begun sketching out your escape plan?"

Claire leaned back in her chair. "I need something stable, so I can have a family someday," she said. "But not boring. Something I can be proud of and really enjoy. Maybe something of my own. I'm willing to work hard—but I won't be stressed, I'll be *passionate*. I want to create a place where people can come together and enjoy themselves," she continued, her gaze growing distant. "Somewhere where people feel connected and loved." She looked around. "Something like this..."

"Hold that thought." Maggie pointed at Claire's drink. "I'm going to get one of those." She got up and walked over toward the counter.

Something like this.

A coffee shop. Of course. Why not? No more slaving away for some corporate giant, no more cubicles and artificial light fixtures. Forget long days at a computer or piles of paperwork. And to not have a boss—oh, yes! No one to throw a wet blanket on her ideas.

Claire began to lose herself in a daydream...

She's awakened by the morning light filtering through her lace curtains. A healthy fern sits on the bedside table where an alarm clock used to rest. What's the point when you set your own schedule? She takes her time getting out of bed, well-rested and excited for the dreamy tasks that await her at her coffee shop.

Neighborhood customers greet her by name as she walks through the door of her shop. She only has time for pleasant hellos as she makes her way to the back to prepare coffee from the far corners of the earth: Ethiopia, Costa Rica, Indonesia.

Someone calls for her, and with pencil in hair she floats over to the bar. A familiar face, the old man from next door, waits for his usual drink before she sits down next to him for a quick chat about Edgar, his beloved tabby. Then she flutters back to her beans, roasts a heavenly batch, and serves it to her customers, who are all salivating from the aromas of a delicious new blend.

In the corner, the university philosophers are bantering eagerly. An eclectically dressed young man is reading Charles Bukowski in a vintage, wingback chair. A pretty young girl is sitting at the window, daydreaming peacefully over a cup of chai.

During the afternoon lull, Claire sits with her friends as they come in and out of the shop. One of the baristas approaches her to have a chat. Claire remembers the days when she would apprehensively approach her previous manager's door. The moment she heard the grumbled, "Come in!" she already felt like a nuisance.

But stress and fear were the dominating forces in her last job; here, she leads with peace and clarity. She welcomes the time with her barista, unbothered, as they digest the events that occurred that day.

She spends the end of her dreamy day finishing up tasks in the back room. She is calm, tired but not exhausted, her day having been the ideal mix of challenge and productivity.

She makes her way to the door and the most beautiful sight greets her. Dusk is breaking over the neighborhood, and her longtime friends are sitting on the couches, drinking her coffee and waiting for her.

"Claire!" they exclaim.

"Hey, guys," she says with a joyful smile.

"We were just discussing going down to the new Japanese restaurant to celebrate Juliah's new job, can you come with us?"

"I'd love to," she says.

It could all be so sweet...

Maggie came back with a drink in hand. "Claire?"

Claire shook her head like she was coming out of a daze, then excitement flashed through her as she met Maggie's eyes.

"I've got it, Maggie. I know what I'm going to do."

***

The next six months evaporated in a flurry of ideas, excitement, loose plans, and wide-eyed faith.

Someone suggested that it might be good for Claire to work at a coffee shop before owning one, but she was too eager to get started, and she knew that her staff could teach her along the way. She'd just find baristas and managers who knew what they were doing.

And it wasn't like she didn't know *anything*.

After all the coffee shops that she'd been to, she understood coffee. She could tell the difference between good coffee and better coffee. She knew about origins and processes and had enjoyed picking the occasional barista's brain, adding to her ever-growing coffee knowledge. She began dreaming up specialty drinks made from interesting varieties and origins.

She'd be a coffee expert in no time.

Besides, she had studied business in college, mostly because she hadn't known what else to do, but she'd always liked assignments where she had to come up with her own business ideas. Moreover, she'd been working at a huge corporation for three years now, and she'd learned a lot there. Maybe the last three years hadn't been wasted after all.

Claire knew what it took to run a business. How hard could it be to run a neighborhood coffee shop?

If she was able to create an atmosphere that drew people into her coffee shop, she knew it could become the neighborhood hangout. Her café would be the community hub where musicians would want to perform. Maybe she would even have a comedy night, and people could realize their dreams of being a stand-up comedian in her very own café. They would say, "It all started at…"

After the plethora of coffee shops that she had visited in her lifetime, she could recall which ones had the best atmosphere and why. She would create the perfect coffee shop, the coffee shop of her dreams.

Plants. There would be plants everywhere. Comfortable chairs, board games, lots of outlets, brick walls. The music playlist would always be updated, and customers would consistently ask, "Hey, what's this song?"

In the summer, the windows would be open, and a soft breeze would come through while people drank iced lattes. In the colder months, the windows might be streaked with rain, but inside would be warm and cozy, and people would be ready to take off their scarf to a warm cup of apple cider.

Claire could fantasize about her coffee shop all day, but she knew she had to be serious about some things. Like coffee equipment. She decided to invest in some of the most expensive equipment to impress her coffee snob friends.

Why not be ready for growth? It would definitely break the bank, but she felt it was an investment. That's what business was all about, right? Taking risks?

The crowds of customers would pay the bills, and money wouldn't be an issue. She would be able to relax and manage her coffee shop, happy and stress-free. She would just have to hold out for a year or so as she built the business.

Now that she had figured out all of the nuts and bolts, all she needed was faith and perseverance.

***

Six months later

No matter how hard Claire scrubbed, the layer of filth on the floor wouldn't budge. She knew she was going to have to retile the bathroom. *Great…another expense.*

Getting up off of her hands and knees, she leaned against the bathroom wall of her coffee shop, breathing out a deep sigh of exhaustion. Her face in the mirror was drawn and her shoulders slumped.

As she leaned there, she realized that even cleaning a bathroom floor could be an escape. Rumbling and growling, the monster of neglected finances waited in her office.

Her father's words echoed through her mind: *Claire, honey, I have to be honest, I'm not sure about this coffee shop thing. But I love you and I know you're a hard worker, so your mom and I agreed to give you a loan to get you started.*

From the beginning, she'd felt doubt radiating from the people around her. Could she really pull this off? She was determined to prove she could. So determined that she couldn't bring herself to admit that she was drowning in seemingly insurmountable debt.

She acted as though her 80-hour work weeks suited her entrepreneurial spirit, but the truth was that she had to keep moving or she'd drown. Some days she felt like she was just working to dig herself into a deeper hole.

Nevertheless, she had promised her dad that she would catch up on the bookkeeping and put a number on this tsunami of debt. She would finish her finances that night.

Scooping up the cleaning equipment, she blew a stray lock of hair out of her face and walked out the bathroom door toward the back. Midnight was approaching, the café was dark, and the chairs had been put up, but the floor still hadn't been swept.

Defeated, she threw the cleaning equipment into the closet and plopped heavily into her office chair. Letting out a long groan, she rubbed her face trying to wake herself up.

The calendar above her computer had the date circled in red Sharpie with "MAGGIE'S BACHELORETTE PARTY" written in all caps. Just hours earlier, Claire had heard the hurt in Maggie's voice on the other line when she had to tell her that she wouldn't be there.

That had stirred up her shame and she immediately became defensive, as if Maggie should have been selfless enough to understand why her best friend couldn't make it to her bachelorette party.

As soon as she'd hung up, one of the baristas had come into the office to ask a question. She'd scurried out quickly when she'd heard the bitterness in Claire's short answer.

Claire, sitting in her office alone, relived the moment and let out another long groan. She sank into her chair, embarrassed and discouraged.

She had become exactly the person she didn't want to be.

She felt like a failure because of her finances, and she felt like a fraud because all of her friends believed she was successful.

Claire was trapped.

***

Two hours later, Claire's eyes were locked on a spreadsheet. She had been staring at the figure for thirty minutes, her eyes moving in and out of focus. If she stared at it long enough, maybe more money would magically appear.

Somehow, over the past year, she had only barely broken even…and really, she wasn't even doing that well because she still wasn't paying herself a salary. Not to mention the loans she had yet to pay back.

It wasn't that she didn't have customers. There were even times when the place was packed. But somehow, she still wasn't producing enough sales. The coffee was good, the ambiance was pretty cool, but something was missing.

Or was this just what life was like for all coffee shop owners? Blissful on the outside but on the inside, nightmarish at best? Could it be that the only people who actually enjoyed coffee shops were the patrons themselves?

Somewhere along the way Claire had lost herself in the tasks, in the revenue, in trying to stay open. There was a time when she'd had a vision for her coffee shop, but she wasn't sure what that looked like anymore.

She wanted it to be a place of gathering, of books and board games. She wanted people to sing and do comedy there. She wanted people to interact and have a great time with one another. She wanted the next great artist to be birthed out of her coffee shop.

But it didn't feel like a community at all. Possibly some of her customers felt it was, but all she felt was exhausted from being pulled in a million different directions.

Why was she even doing this? She didn't know. She'd wanted to escape her old way of life. She'd wanted to own something that she loved. But now she was basically working for free—and how could she ever admit to her friends and family that she was failing?

She got up from her chair and began pacing back and forth, chewing her fingernails.

How could she tell her dad that she was nowhere near her projected goal and there was no hope of paying him back anytime soon? Even worse, she had no idea how to fix this situation.

"*What do I do, what do I do?*" She scanned the room desperately.

Suddenly, a bright yellow sticker caught her eye. The sticker plastered around her water bottle said "La Valeur" in a thick white font.

Ronica Williams was the owner of La Valeur, a successful coffee shop in town. Claire had met her once before at an event in town, and Ronica had surprised Claire with her hospitality.

"If you ever need advice, my door is always open," she had said to Claire.

Why hadn't Claire taken her up on that? Was it pride? Or maybe she had doubted that someone as successful and regal as Ronica had really meant it? Was there even a chance that Ronica could help her now that she was this deep?

It was the only light Claire saw at this point. She decided to call her in the morning.

Chapter 2: The Meeting

"Hey, Ronica!" Claire fumbled nervously with a pen in her hand as she spoke into the phone, a less-than-confident smile on her face. "It's Claire Wallace, the owner of The Haunt." She nodded her head a few times enthusiastically. "Yeah, exactly! So, actually, I was calling you because you offered to give me some pointers about running a coffee shop."

Her anxiety pushed her out of her office chair, and she began pacing again. "I was hoping, if you're still open to it, that I could take you up on that offer sometime soon?"

For the first time in months, she felt something like relief, and she stopped pacing. "Great, thanks so much, Ronica, that sounds great. Tomorrow, 3 p.m., your shop."

***

"Hey, Claire, welcome."

Ronica waved Claire over to the table where she was sitting near the coffee bar. Claire noticed how Ronica's shoulders were back and she was sitting up straight, exuding confidence.

"How's it going?" Ronica smiled at her. "What can I do for you?"

Claire had been to La Valeur before she'd started her own shop, but now she took in La Valeur's decor from a different perspective.

The café felt bright and spacious, with lots of white, modern furniture accented in gold. Her eyes were drawn to a tasteful display of artwork from the local high school. There was a rare mix of integrity and hospitality in this place.

"Oh, I have some coffee for you here, if you'd like some." Ronica pushed a cup across the table.

"Sure, I'd like that," Claire took a seat across from the coffee shop owner. Her eyes lit up as she took a sip. "Wow, that's some good coffee."

"Thank you." Ronica laughed.

"To answer your question, it's going all right." Claire looked into her coffee.

"Really?"

"Yeah…" Claire's gaze drifted around the café.

"Claire, how's it really going?"

Ronica's tone was kind but firm, and Claire knew she wasn't going to get away with pretending things were all right. Her eyes began to glisten, and her throat went dry. It suddenly became very hard to talk. She decided that she'd rather be silent than start bawling in front of Ronica.

Ronica put her hands down on the table in front of her. "Claire, when I was starting out in coffee, I had all the knowledge. I had worked with coffee farmers myself and watched the fruit go from being picked off the trees to being turned into some of the best-known coffee in the world. I have a master's in business administration. I even have relatives who farmed coffee before some family disputes brought them to the United States.

"I thought if anyone would be able to have a successful coffee shop, it would be me. My family and friends all believed in me, and they were excited to see me open up a shop in town. Some of them even invested in the coffee shop.

"But after a year, it was pretty clear that I was not doing well. I was disconnected from my employees, my fiancé and I were on the verge of breaking up, my body was racked with stress. I even comforted myself with pastries from my own shop until I had put on ten pounds!" She laughed and continued.

"And on top of that, I felt like I was failing—failing my family, friends, and my community. I isolated myself because I didn't want to face people, and my only companion was an underlying shame that I couldn't even face. It was terrible."

This sounded familiar. Claire hung on every word. "What happened?"

Ronica lifted her head proudly. "I got help. I was unsure, but someone I trusted recommended a coffee shop management course to me. I swallowed my pride and listened to what they had to say. It was hard for me to admit that although I had an MBA, there were major gaps in my ability to lead a business. I realized that I needed better systems and processes in place, but even more importantly, I needed to be clear on my vision and my purpose. I needed to be clear on my culture."

"I guess I haven't thought much about my coffee shop's culture..." Claire was dubious. "I mean, I don't know if that's the most important aspect. Isn't it all about the finances and the location and the customers?"

Ronica nodded to show Claire she understood.

Claire, feeling more comfortable, began to speak. "At first, it was all about finding the best location, but when I couldn't get the one I wanted, I settled for one in a different neighborhood. I had to pay more for the construction than I originally thought; there were some problems with the drainpipes..."

Ronica nodded knowingly. Claire continued.

"That wiped out my savings, so before we even opened, I was falling behind. After that, it was just more debt and more debt. I tried to fix it by changing what we sold, changing the furniture, changing our menu. Nothing has worked." Claire swallowed. "If things don't turn around soon, I'm in big trouble." She looked away and tears began to stream down her cheek.

Ronica reached across the table and rested her hand on Claire's arm, letting her cry.

Finally, Claire uttered a strained, "Is it too far gone?"

"Listen, Claire, this might not be as hopeless as you think." Compassion glowed in Ronica's eyes. "I'm not going to make any empty promises, and I'm not going to tell you that implementing the changes you need to make will be easy. But I have seen a lot of coffee shop owners turn things around. People who were in your same situation."

Claire grabbed the napkin from underneath her mug and dabbed her eyes and nose. Her face was blotchy and red.

Ronica took her hand off of Claire's arm and leaned back. "But I can't do it for you. I can tell you what to do, and how to do it, but I cannot promise you success. This is only going to work if you put what I show you into practice."

Claire put down the napkin, nodding slightly to show she understood.

"Well, it just so happens that one of the workshops will be beginning in two weeks, and I'm going to facilitate it. It's a two-step process that begins with a workshop where you gain clarity on your culture and strategy and learn what you need to do to improve your coffee shop. Then, in the second phase, you will implement what you learn in the workshop with a cohort of other coffee shop owners."

Claire was skeptical. Could clarifying her culture and strategy really help her? Was that really the solution to her problems? It seemed so abstract and touchy-feely to her.

And how could she possibly afford another expense right now?

"Thank you so much for offering your services, Ronica," Claire said politely, "but I just don't know how I could possibly invest more time and money right now." She hesitated, not quite ready to let the dream of success go. "I mean, could this really help me?"

Ronica leaned in, her voice confident. "I know what you're thinking Claire. Trust me, I was there. It seems too simple, doesn't it? But that's why it works. You're not wrong to believe that things like furniture and pricing and coffee are essential to your business—they are. But the undisciplined pursuit of these things without a solid culture and strategy is burning you out. It's because you don't understand what's going on beneath that. It's not sustainable, and it's not aligned with who you are and who you are serving."

Claire thought about it for a moment, digesting what Ronica was saying.

Ronica continued, "Listen, the owner of Sweet Jay Coffee on the other side of town took the course last year. He's a friendly man, give him a ring. This is a lot of time and money, and I want you to be sure before you sign up."

Ronica wrote down a number and a name on a sticky note, which she handed to Claire.

"Give it some more thought when you go home tonight."

"Okay, I'll think about it," Claire said, looking down and fiddling with the sticky note.

"And if you decide you want to do it, give me a call, and we'll get together one last time before the workshop so I can give you some more information," Ronica offered.

"I really appreciate you, Ronica." Claire began to get emotional again. She still wasn't sure about this workshop, but she was grateful for Ronica's kindness. "I've felt so alone."

"You are far from it," said Ronica matter-of-factly.

***

Claire held the sticky note from Ronica between her fingers. She was back in her office, trying to be productive but failing. Her mind was swirling with what-ifs and decisions galore.

Before she could talk herself out of it, she picked up the phone and dialed the number.

The line was ringing.

Gosh, what was she going to sa—

"Hello?" said an older man's voice.

Too late.

"Hi, there. This is Claire Wallace. I own a coffee shop in town. I'm not sure if Ronica from La Valeur told you I'd be calling you. Is this the owner of Sweet Jay Coffee?"

"Oh, hi, Claire. Yes, it sure is. This is Jeff." The voice, pleasant and true, reminded her of her grandpa, who'd grown up among the cornfields of Nebraska. "Ronica did tell me you'd be calling. How's it going?"

"Hey, Jeff. It's going, well—erm, actually…yeah, not so great. Which is why I wanted to talk to you. I'm thinking about taking the course that Ronica helps teach. She said you took it yourself…?" Claire's voice trailed off.

Jeff's voice was bright and full of energy. "I sure did. Oh, let me see, it was about a year ago now."

"Okay, wow. So how was it, did it help you?" Claire held her breath, waiting for his answer.

"Oh yeah, it definitely did," Jeff said.

Hope flared in Claire's chest.

Jeff continued. "You know, Claire, I really do understand why you're calling and asking because I was also hesitant. I'm a really practical guy, you know. I love coffee and I love fixing things, but purpose, culture–I hadn't given those any thought."

On the other end of the line, Claire nodded. She could relate.

Jeff continued, "I trusted Ronica, though. She's a brilliant woman and obviously quite successful in our industry, and so even when I didn't fully understand, I tried my best to 'do the hard work,' as they put it, and kept pressing on. Eventually, it made a real difference."

"What changed?" Claire was on the edge of her seat.

"Well, definitely my employees. Once they understood, they had more energy. Probably because they finally understood what the hell we were doing over here. Sure, some people couldn't get on board, but they weren't really the people I wanted around anyway, you know what I'm saying? And I was just less stressed. I had good managers who understood what we were trying to do. I had customers who really liked what we were going for, and they were generally impressed and happy with their experience. I feel so much calmer now that everyone knows what our values are, the things that are non-negotiable for me, and they know that that's how we behave.

"Most importantly, I've been able to step away from the shop for two days a week and spend time with my grandkids and my wife and whoever else. Before, I was always here because it felt like I was the only thing keeping it together."

Claire's eyes were wide. "Wow, Jeff, I'm so happy for you. That's great."

"Yeah, it's really something. I'm happy to be the owner of this fine establishment." Jeff paused. "If you're willing to dig in, Claire, go for it. Make your dreams come true."

Claire's eyes started to water again—why was she getting emotional? Her heart felt so tender these days. "Thank you so much, Jeff. I'd like to stop by sometime and check out Sweet Jay."

"You're always welcome, Claire."
"Thank you, see you later."
Click.

***

Claire sat in the light of the lamp on her bedside table.

Her mood had shifted over the past hours from defeated to puzzled to unmistakably hopeful, as she thought about her talks with Ronica and Jeff that day.

She didn't really understand it, but there was definitely something going on here.

Her mind began to wander as she stared out her bedroom window. The streetlights cast pockets of warm light onto the road below her. What would it be like to be debt-free? To pay back all the people she owed money to? Just the thought was so light and so freeing that some of the tension drained from her shoulders. Claire took a deep breath and exhaled.

She had to try.

She picked up her phone.

"Hey, Ronica, it's Claire. Sorry for calling you so late. I, uh, talked to Jeff, and yeah, it seems like whatever you're talking about really made a difference for him. And well, I'd love to be in Jeff's position." She laughed. "So, when you get this message, give me a ring. I'd love to set up a time to talk with you. Okay, goodnight."

Chapter 3: Getting Started

Ronica was standing outside of The Haunt early the next morning. In her trench coat and with her excellent posture, Claire imagined she looked a little like an army general. Like someone who had come out of a fight victoriously.

Claire jumped out of her car, jittery with excitement and nerves.

"Hey, Ronica!" she exclaimed with a smile.

"How are you doing, Claire?" Ronica observed her with keen eyes. "You look a little more energetic this fine morning."

Claire walked up to the door of the shop, fumbling with the keys in the lock and laughing a little. "Do I? That's good news." She pushed the door open for Ronica.

Claire knew what Ronica was talking about; she already felt a little different. It's funny what a little hope can do to a person.

Ronica stepped in and looked around the front room as Claire pulled some chairs off of tables and strode behind the bar.

"Let me make you something," said Claire, turning on machines and lights.

"Sure, I'll take a cup of your house roast," said Ronica.

Claire brewed two cups of the day's featured coffee and joined Ronica at a table, sweeping her hair behind her ears. Alert, attentive, ready.

Ronica picked up her cup with a nod of thanks. "Okay. So, today let's just talk about what the next seven months are going to look like, and I'll answer any questions you may have."

Claire nodded. "That sounds great, fill me in."

Ronica took a sip of the coffee. "Hey, not bad, Claire!" she said with a grin.

Claire's cheeks warmed at the praise. "Thank you."

"Okay, the workshop goes for six days, and the main purpose of the class is to gain the clarity you need to move forward. Each day, we'll tackle some big questions that are very specific to you and your coffee shop. The goal is that by the end of the workshop, you are confident about your answers to these questions."

Claire nodded. "That seems straightforward enough."

Ronica continued, "Once the class is over, you and your classmates will form a 'cohort' of sorts. Usually, we do a Facebook group or something, and together you'll be walked through a six-month implementation process."

Claire perked up and adjusted in her chair. She was intrigued, excited, and slightly nervous about the idea of walking through such a vulnerable process with other coffee shop owners.

"This will be invaluable to you," Ronica assured her. "You'll find encouragement, and you'll be able to encourage others who are on the same journey with you."

"Okay, that's awesome. Can you explain a little more what the implementation process looks like?"

"Sure," Ronica said. "Basically, all you need to know now is that you'll create systems that are built on the answers you give in the class. Then, it'll be about communicating your culture and implementing those systems with your employees."

Claire sat back in her chair. "Okay, great. Sounds good."

She didn't fully understand yet, but she had already decided that she was going to trust the process. What she currently lacked in details, she was beginning to make up for in hope and confidence.

"Do you have any questions?" Ronica asked.

"No, not right now," Claire answered.

"All right, well since we have some time, let me ask you some questions."

"Okay." Claire sat up a little straighter.

Ronica's tone was serious. "Why are you really doing this?"

"What, the coffee shop?" Claire said.

"Yes, what motivated you to open up a coffee shop?"

Claire thought a moment. "Uhm, well, it sounded like a good idea and I hated my job." She laughed as she looked over toward the wall.

"I wanted to earn money doing something I liked." She shrugged and looked back over at Ronica.

Ronica nodded. "Okay sure, but you could have done a lot of different things. I mean, why a coffee shop? What is the dream, Claire?"

Claire gave a short laugh. "To pay off my debt. To have a day off. To hang out with my friends again."

Ronica gave her a knowing smile. "You're still in survival mode," she said. "I'm talking long-term. Beyond all your problems right now, what was *the* dream?"

Claire was struck. The hard shell of ice around her spirit seemed to crack a bit, reminding her that the dream, which she'd almost forgotten about, was still there, under it all.

"Wow, yeah, *the* dream." Claire's eyes began to wander around the room.

She gazed at her cozy living room furniture in the center of the room, surrounded by tables and chairs. It was true; she'd had a dream once.

Claire looked back at Ronica, who was waiting patiently. "I wanted to create a hub. Like a place where people would come and perform. You know, like open mic nights and whatnot." She chuckled, feeling a little sheepish. "I even had an idea for a comedy night where people could try their hand at stand-up."

Her eyes got a faraway look; that daydreamer was coming back out. "I imagined that this place would be full. Full of people drinking chai and espresso, watching others perform. There would be a sense of camaraderie. It would be nice and warm in here, and people would meet one another from the neighborhood."

Ronica smiled. "It sounds like you are motivated by creating belonging."

Claire looked back at Ronica, her eyes bright and slightly moist. "Yes, belonging. That was the dream."

"Wonderful." Ronica's voice was sincere. "Okay, and what about your values?"

"My values?"

"Yeah, like how will your staff treat each other? Your behaviors." Ronica was gesturing with her hands to emphasize her point. "What pleases you when it's done and disappoints you when it's not done? What do you truly value?"

Claire gave her a wry smile. "Well, I definitely value hard work, when everything gets done around here."

"Sure, everyone is happy when their employees do what they're supposed to do, but what separates you from other coffee shops?" Ronica pressed. "What makes your values different from other coffee shops?"

Claire understood. She chewed on it a bit. "Hmmm, what makes us different…"

When Claire had been in sixth grade, she'd felt like a fish out of water. Looking back on it, she was sure that almost everyone felt like a fish out of water—except maybe the exceptionally good-looking fish.

But Claire had moved to a new state that summer. She didn't know anyone at her new school and was just starting to realize that she didn't really know herself.

The first few months were rough. She was overwhelmed on the school bus, quiet during class, alone during lunch, and reclusive after school.

And then she'd met Grace.

Grace had been an angel during a time of darkness. Claire sometimes wished she could find this girl now or find her mother and thank her for raising a daughter with such a pure heart.

The day she met Grace stood out in her memory so clearly, even after all this time. It was the beginning of another awkward day, and to make matters worse, she was running late. Which meant everyone at the bus stop watched her run down the street toward them for at least two minutes before she made it, huffing and puffing as the school bus pulled up.

She sat down toward the middle of the bus, alone and defeated. No one said a word to her. Shocker.

The school bus began to pull away. Just as she was putting in her headphones, a bright-eyed girl plopped down next to her.

Startled, Claire released the headphone in her left hand, and it swung down toward her lap.

The girl laughed and flashed perfectly straight teeth—post braces. "Sorry, didn't mean to scare ya! I'm Grace, what's your name?"

"Hi, I'm Claire." Claire smiled.

Grace was in the eighth grade. She was the rare breed of person who had people close to her but didn't cling to them like the other kids. She didn't always sit next to Claire either, but it seemed like she always did when Claire really needed it.

Sometimes she would sit with Claire during lunch, sometimes they would walk home together after school.

Since reflecting on it, Claire was sure that Grace saw how desperately Claire needed a friend, but she never said that. Yet it worked. Especially because Grace was one of those confident and good-looking fish, so the fact that she treated Claire like a normal person made Claire *feel* like a normal person.

She had hope, and it was all she needed to open her eyes to the world around her. Friends came more naturally after that, and slowly but surely, she began to pursue interests at school, like theater.

Claire sat up and looked at Ronica with confidence. "Inclusiveness. The kind that treats everyone with value and makes sure that everyone is accounted for."

"Sounds like a great value for a community hub." Ronica leaned back and comfortably crossed her arms over her chest.

"Yeah, it does, doesn't it?" Claire smiled.

"So, it's unrealistic for us to go through all of the questions today, and we'll do that in the class anyway, but I wanted to get your mind going and activate some of those old dreams again," Ronica explained.

Claire smiled a smile without defeat. It was a quiet strength that was coming back out.

Ronica took one last swig of the coffee. "All right, Claire, I'm off. Here's a flier for the workshop with the link to sign up and pay. The address is on there with the date and time." She gave Claire a wink. "See you there."

Ronica headed out the door just as Claire felt a low vibration in her pocket. She pulled her phone out and looked at the caller ID.

"Oh, man." Taking a deep breath, she stood up. "Hey, Dad."

Claire's dad wasn't tyrannical nor was he an angry man. In fact, he was very calm most of the time. And yet his words could bite like an Arctic wind on bare skin.

For as long as Claire could remember, she had only heard him apologize for minor incidents, like bumping elbows with a woman at the grocery store. But he never apologized for putting fear into the people around him. He had no patience for other people's mistakes or shortcomings, and it showed.

He had been pretty open about how he didn't approve of Claire's adventures after college, and he had been the most pleased when she settled into her high-paying corporate job.

When she decided to open the coffee shop, she hated the idea of asking him to invest in the business, but he was one of the wealthiest people she knew...and he was her father, right?

It wasn't easy and sometimes she wished that he had said no because now she lived with the constant shame of having not yet been able to pay him back.

"How's it going?"

Even his greeting sounded disapproving.

"All right, what's going on with you?" She braced herself for what was certainly coming next.

"Well, I was just looking over those numbers you sent me." He paused. "It wasn't what I expected."

"I know, I know—" she began, but he cut her off.

"How much longer am I going to have to wait on this haphazard business plan?"

She squeezed her eyes shut as she tried to keep herself from saying something she'd regret. She thought about how terrible it is to owe money to someone who demeans you.

Calming herself, she replied, "I'm already working on a better business plan, and in six months you will see that it's only up from here. I have to go, Dad, but you'll get your money back and then some."

"Okay, honey, I'm going to believe that." His tone was full of doubt. "But if it doesn't look better in six months, I'm not going to be happy, Claire."

"Don't worry. It will. Okay, bye, Dad. Nice talking to you." She hung up the phone.

Claire let out a deep breath and looked around her coffee shop. Man, she really hoped this was going to work.

Part II
Gaining Clarity

Chapter 4: Vulnerability

Claire checked the number on the building once more and reached for the door. Her nerves were tingling at a low frequency, making her uneasy.

It wasn't that she was socially awkward—in fact, she normally would have said that she was quite good with people. Perhaps it was the fact that her social interactions these days were limited to behind her coffee bar...or maybe it was that her self-confidence had taken a hard hit since opening shop.

Truthfully, much of what she used to identify with, the parts of her life that made up her self-image, were now absent. As long as she had been either benefiting society, making enough money to do the things she loved, or at least having a good time, she'd felt successful.

But now she didn't feel like she was doing any of those things.

She rarely had the chance to meet up with her friends anymore. If she was being honest, she could have made the time, but she was beginning to avoid them. If she didn't see them then she didn't have to fake success or reveal that she was failing.

She had always prided herself on her ability to make "it" happen. If there was a will, there was a way! And yet now, with the greatest venture of her life, she had run out of ways and was losing the will. The apprehension and doubt in her dad's voice still echoed in the back of her mind. But maybe this was going to be different. There was hope—there was definitely hope.

And nervousness. Lots of nervousness.

Claire's eyes moved quickly down the directory as she looked for Conference Room 3. Found it. Her heels clacked on the tile floor as she made her way down the hallway.

Would she recognize anyone there besides Ronica? It was selfish because it would mean they needed help too, but she almost hoped people would be there who looked like they were way ahead of her but were actually in the same boat.

Conference Room 3 was written over the door in metallic letters. Claire took a deep breath and walked into a long room, which was set up conference-style. About ten people were sitting in chairs facing the front where Ronica was standing in a long, burnt-orange dress.

Ronica looked up at Claire with a smile then continued her conversation with a man sitting at the front. Claire made her way toward an open seat, exchanging shy smiles with some of the other people in the room.

She sat down next to a man who looked like he was around her age. He had a light brown fedora on his head and an impressive dark mustache coupled with a short beard. His button-down shirt was undone nearly to the middle of his chest, and he was wearing Oxford shoes with jeans that were cuffed on the end.

He looked up as Claire was sitting down. "Hey, how's it going?" he said as he held out his hand. "My name's Griffin."

Claire shook his hand. "Hi, Griffin. Claire."

"Where's your coffee shop at?" His eyes were curious.

"In the southeast part of town."

"Oh, right on. I'm pretty close by, in the industrial district."

"Cool, what's the name of it?" Claire asked.

"Cuppa," said Griffin. "It's what Australians call a cup of coffee. I spent a lot of time there about two years ago." His gaze softened. "I miss it. What a beautiful place."

"Wow, that's amazing." Claire was about to say more when there was a tangible shift in the room. Conversations suddenly died out, and the audience directed their attention toward the front.

"Hey, everyone, welcome to our Coffee Shop Success Workshop." Ronica beamed at the audience. "It's important for you to understand that you're not coming here just to listen to me share ideas. We're going to do a lot of hard work together, and it's going to take courage and transparency. What you get out of this workshop will be determined by the level at which you participate and the extent to which you're willing to be honest with yourself."

Without moving her head, Claire darted her eyes around the room curiously, trying to get a sense of how the other participants were feeling.

"It's nice to see some familiar faces." Ronica glanced around the room. "So, obviously, many of you know that I'm Ronica Williams, and I'm the owner of the coffee shop La Valeur, on the west side of town."

La Valeur sounded so much more elegant when Ronica pronounced it with a perfect French accent.

"I took a class similar to this one almost four years ago, and it helped me get to where I'm at today," Ronica continued. "Which, of course, means that La Valeur is doing well, but more importantly—" she paused to emphasize her point "—*I'm* doing well."

A smattering of applause broke out around the room.

"But I wasn't always." She looked at class with no trace of embarrassment. "I wasn't a fool when I started. It's not like I had no idea that it was going to be hard work. And I *definitely* worked hard. There can be no doubts about that. And yet, even with patience, I wasn't achieving what I desired to achieve. Ultimately, I wanted to give back to the community, and I felt terrible that I wasn't anywhere close to that goal."

Ronica began to slowly walk around the room as she was talking. "I was working way too many hours. Leaving bright and early to open the shop and coming home late after closing."

She stopped and swept the room with her gaze. "But that wasn't the real problem."

The room grew completely silent and the audience leaned forward slightly in their chairs as if everyone knew they were about to receive something precious.

"I'm not proud to admit this, but it was destroying my life," Ronica admitted. "I was stuck, and I didn't know how to get out of it except by working like a maniac. All of the time, as hard as I could, even though I was going nowhere, like a hamster on a wheel."

Ronica looked directly at Griffin. "I mean, wouldn't you have worked as hard as I did if you felt like everything depended on it? If you felt your reputation, your dignity, your place in your community, your savings, all those years invested, depended on it?"

Griffin shifted slightly in his seat to relieve the tension, and Claire saw some people noticeably wince as if they were reliving their own story.

Ronica continued, "And I want to add that during this time, La Valeur was becoming really popular. We were packed consistently. So it's not that we weren't successful on some level, but financially, we were not doing great."

Lots of nods around the room. Someone said, "Mm-hmm."

Ronica stopped on one side of the conference room and, looking out the window, she said, "There was one night when my fiancé—my husband now, by the grace of God—we got into a huge fight. He had stayed by my side faithfully for over a year of that madness, and he was finally getting to a point where he couldn't handle it anymore. I was a different person. I was completely absent, completely exhausted, completely frantic."

She turned back around and began making her way to the front of the room.

"I was so at the end of my rope that when he confronted me, I lost my temper and told him to leave. He could hear the sound of china breaking as he was walking out the door. I just needed to take out my anger on something, and that night it was the dishes."

A pause. No one moved; all eyes were on Ronica.

"And that's when I got help," she said. "And that's when hope started entering the picture."

A woman with glasses and dark hair pulled back in a ponytail said, "Thank you for sharing that with us, Ronica. I would never have thought you went through something like that because of La Valeur."

Ronica nodded and leaned into the palms of her hands on the table in front of her. "Thanks, Jennifer. But that's why I'm so passionate about helping all of you. There is a way forward." She said it defiantly, stirring up hope in the room.

Claire stared at Jennifer curiously. She looked so familiar…where did Claire know this woman from?

Ronica interrupted her thoughts. "Now listen, everyone, we're going to be sharing some very personal and real parts of our life with each other. We have to if we're going to make this work. But first, I need you to sign this agreement."

She began passing some papers out from her tote bag. "If there's any hope of moving forward, the first step is creating a space where we can be completely honest and vulnerable with each other. But if I'm going to ask you to be this vulnerable, I want you all to be assured that what is said here *stays* here."

Claire looked down at the paper that was put in front of her: CONFIDENTIALITY AGREEMENT.

"Everyone please sign to promise that what is said in this room stays in this room."

No one hesitated. The soft scratch of pens on paper as people signed their agreements was the only sound out in the room.

"Also," Ronica continued, "what I just did, being vulnerable, that's what you're going to have to do with your employees when you go back to them after this workshop. You're going to need to create some trust within your group, but the only way you can do that, is if you yourself are vulnerable with them and with each other."

Everyone nodded.

Ronica smiled. "All right, who's familiar with the Meyers Briggs test?"

***

According to the Myers Briggs test, Claire was an ENFP, which meant that she was charismatic and a dreamer. Someone who loved grand ideas but wasn't great at administrative tasks.

Shocker.

She had learned that her new friend Griffin was an ISFP, an adventurer who loved to challenge social norms. For him, coming back to the city to watch over his aging parents and start up a coffee shop was one of the most mature decisions he could make.

Griffin had been impressively candid with Claire about the reason how he had detested the idea of settling down until this moment. He feared the mundane. Adventure had been wrapped into his identity, and now that he was sitting still, he had to answer deeper questions about his inherent value. He struggled with executing long-term goals and found himself getting lost in the present moment. His coffee shop had suffered because of it.

A man in a polo shirt and khaki pants named Stephen had not been as open about his weaknesses. According to him, things were going all right at his coffee shop. It confused Claire because on the one hand, he was at this class; he must need some kind of help. On the other hand, he seemed indifferent about the state of his business. Was he just having a hard time opening up, or was he actually doing fine? She couldn't tell, but she had a hunch that there was more going on there.

Claire climbed the stairs to her apartment door, putting her keys in the hole and turning the knob as she pushed into the door.

Pajama time.

Strangely, she felt as if a weight had lifted when Ronica had shared her story in more detail today. Since this coffee adventure had begun, Claire had been comparing herself to women like Ronica, and deep down she had felt like the loser of the coffee world. Now she was seeing that not only was she not the only one but that what she was going through wasn't even that unusual.

Claire sat on her couch in her softest pajamas with a mug of herbal tea in her hands and stared at the wall in front of her. She absently blew on her tea while her mind began to wander. She thought about Maggie, her dearest friend, and wondered if she had ruined their relationship.

Maggie had been one of her greatest cheerleaders and had encouraged her time and time again to chase after her dreams. But she had let Maggie down. Not because she was failing but because she had chosen to isolate herself instead of opening up about her burdens.

Stress, shame, and fear had swindled her out of a friendship.

And yet, ever since she had been honest with Ronica, that shame was beginning to fade, and a faint but tangible sense of worthiness and hope were coming to life.

Claire took a deep breath and reached for her phone.

"Maggie Reynolds" read the phone number in her contact list.

Claire looked up and thought for a moment, then she quickly dialed the number, tapping her foot anxiously.

Ring. Ring. Ring.

"Hello?" Maggie's voice rang through the phone with a hint of curiosity.

Slightly uncomfortable, Claire said, "Hey, Mags, what are you up to?"

"Hey, Claire, not much." Maggie sounded more curious than angry, which gave Claire hope. "Just about to turn in for the night."

"Okay, yeah, I thought so, uhm…could you talk for just like ten minutes? I need to apologize to you," she added quickly.

"All right…"

Claire took a deep breath and began. "So, I haven't been completely honest with you, Maggie, and I'm really sorry. And I don't want to make excuses. More than anything, I just want to apologize because I really let you down, Mags. I'm so sorry for how I've been treating you." Claire let urgency creep into her voice, hoping to make Maggie understand. "I've actually really been struggling with the coffee shop, and I was so ashamed that I didn't want to tell you. I've been so stressed out, and it's taken me powering through every moment to keep my head above water. The truth is that I really wanted to make time for our friendship. I don't know how a person can feel so lonely and want to hide so much at the same time."

"Oh, Claire, I didn't know you were having such a hard time." Maggie sounded concerned.

"How could you? I was avoiding everyone because I felt I needed to be at The Haunt every second I had, and I couldn't face you guys with how stressed I was."

"Well, Claire, you know I'm here for the good, the bad, and the ugly. But you have to *let me* be here for you."

"I know, I know. I know that now." She'd forgotten how dependable Maggie was. "You've always been there for me. I don't know why I was isolating myself so much." Claire burst into tears.

"Hey, it's all right, Claire, you're not alone. Maybe we can find you some help?" Maggie's voice was soothing.

"I think I did," she sniffed, collecting herself. "Thank goodness. You know the coffee place La Valeur?"

"Yeah, I know it."

"Well, the owner, Ronica Williams, has a workshop that specifically helps coffee shop owners." Claire laughed. "I'm hoping it's going to change things. But either way, I'm feeling better."

"That's great, Claire. So, you're going to make it to the wedding, then?" Maggie asked.

"I wouldn't miss it for the world," Claire said with absolute certainty.

"Great. Okay, I'm going to turn in, Claire. I'm glad you called. Let's get together soon, all right?"

"I'd love to." Claire smiled.

"All right, bye now."

"Goodnight, Mags."

Claire let out a deep breath. Freedom. She was starting to feel more like herself as she faced the shame and secrets that had been haunting her.

As she headed to bed, she felt stronger, more up to the task.

Maybe she would be honest with her dad next. She was really going to need strength for that one. But for the first time in a long time, it didn't feel impossible.

She clicked off the light.

Chapter 5: Culture

Claire's peace was short-lived. Steam was practically rising from her head as she seethed and murmured in the car on her way to day two of class.

All right, that was it—she was going to do something about this.

Claire quickly put on her left blinker and made a spontaneous detour.

The Haunt was pretty quiet as Claire walked in, with only two university students sitting by the window on their laptops.

Claire walked up to a young woman behind the bar in thick-rimmed glasses. "Hey, Violet. Is Amber here?"

"Hey, Claire, yeah she's here," Violet replied. "She's taking care of some things in the back."

"Great, I just need to chat with her for a moment."

Violet nodded, her curious eyes following her to the back.

Claire didn't have a lot of time before the workshop started, but she had to make sure nothing like this happened again. Not this week. Not ever.

Amber was standing in the back on her phone, leaning against a counter. When she saw Claire, she threw her phone into her back pocket and stood up straight.

"Hey, Claire, what's going on? I didn't think you'd be here today."

Amber was a freshman at the university in town and clearly felt that working as a barista gave her a hip, edgy vibe. Claire wasn't unsympathetic. Freshman year of college is a merciless time for women who gain their self-confidence from being a part of something "cool." But the sympathy stopped when Amber treated other people as less than.

"Hey, Amber, will you take a seat with me for a moment?" Claire said. "I need to talk to you about something real quick."

"Okay…" said Amber, obviously suspicious as she sat down at the backroom table with Claire.

Claire began. "So, yesterday my cousin came into the shop and told me about a very unpleasant interaction that she had with you in the late morning. Do you know what I'm talking about?" she asked, reminding herself to stay calm and be fair.

"Uhm, no…?"

"Okay, well this is what she told me. She said she walked up to the bar, excited to check out her cousin's new coffee shop, and the barista was nowhere to be found. She waited for a minute when she noticed you had an apron around your waist, but you were sitting at a table with a boy your age. You made eye contact with her and then you begrudgingly got up and went behind the bar. She then asked you what a con panna was, and she said you laughed and said, 'You don't know what a con panna is?' as you made eye contact with the boy at the table. It was pretty obvious to her that you were trying to impress him. After she got her coffee from you, she watched as a group of college students came in and you proceeded to explain almost every item on the menu to them, with not even the slightest hint of mockery. In fact, you seemed happy they asked."

Amber was silent.

"Did this happen, Amber?" Claire was keeping a tight rein on her emotions, trying not to let Amber see how angry she really was.

Amber leaned back in her chair casually, looking around at the wall and then back at Claire. "Well, that seems a little dramatic to me."

It would have been one thing if this had been a review and Claire hadn't known the customer personally, but her cousin was an extremely rational and level-headed person. If anything, she'd probably downplayed the event for fear of getting Amber in trouble.

"Listen, Amber, maybe this is my own fault because I never made this crystal clear to you, but at The Haunt, we treat *all* our customers with respect, and we go out of our way to make sure everyone feels comfortable." Claire paused and put her hands together in front of her on the table. "*Always*. Please, don't let it happen again."

"Okay, you got it, boss." Amber's voice was unenthusiastic.

"Thank you." Claire got up from her seat, still angry and slightly uneasy. What she really wanted to do was let Amber go, but mercy cried out to give her one more chance.

Plus, Amber did make really great coffee.

It did make her wonder, though—how many other times had this happened?

"Bye, Violet," said Claire as she walked out the door. She jumped into her car and raced off toward Ronica's workshop.

***

From across the table, Griffin gave her a friendly wave. "Hey, Claire."

"Hey, Griffin." She forced a smile as she sat down.

"Welcome, everyone," Ronica said at the front of the classroom. "All right, let's get started. So, the first three questions that we will be addressing in today's class will be about culture, and they will help you clarify your own culture. But before we get into those questions, how do you know if you have a culture problem?"

Ronica moved to the whiteboard behind her and began writing.

These are five symptoms of a culture problem.

1. *The people you want to stay are leaving and the people you want to leave are staying*
2. *Problems repeat themselves*
3. *Walking into your coffee shop is normally not a positive experience*
4. *You're working too many hours*
5. *Your personal relationships are being affected by your business*

Nods could be seen around the room, and Claire took a deep breath, identifying with far too many items on the list.

Ronica smiled at Claire. "What *should* be happening is that the people who don't fit the values of your coffee shop are naturally leaving, problems solve themselves, and walking into your coffee shop is the best part of your day."

The room was silent.

Ronica continued, "Take your time with these questions, they are incredibly important. Your culture will form the foundation that everything else is built on. Beginning with question number one: Why are you doing this?"

Ronica began pacing around the room. "Simon Sinek says, 'People don't buy what you do, they buy *why* you do it.' I want to feel inspired when I hear these answers. More importantly, you and your employees should be inspired. It should be slightly grandiose. Some of you more practical people might have a hard time with this."

"You mean it can't be to make money and drink coffee all day?" Jennifer joked.

The class chuckled.

"If that's really why you have a coffee shop, Jennifer, then you might be better suited for a roastery," Ronica said, a twinkle in her eye. "No one wants to see your greedy butt running a customer service business."

Jennifer suddenly turned serious. "No, that's not it for me. I started Obsidian because I saw a need for innovation in the coffee industry, and I want to give people the latest and greatest coffee."

Ronica nodded approvingly. "Very inspirational. Excellent answer."

Of course, Obsidian! That was Jennifer's coffee shop. Claire knew that she'd looked familiar.

Jennifer had been featured in an article in a popular coffee publication that covered some of her game-changing work in the industry. She had also been the winner of a few national coffee competitions. Claire had been intrigued to find out that this woman lived in her city.

Why was *she* here?

Claire figured she would hear about it later and got back to the task at hand. She thought back to her previous conversation with Ronica and about the passion and hope that had sparked as a result. She wrote down on her paper, "To create a space where people feel accepted and connected."

She stared at the paper and couldn't resist the feeling of enthusiasm that bubbled up inside of her.

"Okay, next question," Ronica went on. "What do you want to accomplish in the next ten years? If you have a ten-year plan, a one-year plan is easy. It doesn't matter how fast you go, all that matters is you know where you're going, you're going in the right direction, and you're making progress toward that goal. I want a visual picture. If all your dreams came true, what would your business look like?"

Claire loved this question—it fit right in with her daydreamer persona. She looked over at Griffin, who was staring blankly at the wall, scratching his head.

In ten years...she would want to have shops in multiple neighborhoods around the city. In every neighborhood that needed more camaraderie, that needed a place where people could come together.

Maybe four different cafés. And they would all be known for their open mic nights and comedy nights. The culture would be so set there that people would know that they'd be accepted when they walked through the door and would feel empowered to talk to strangers.

Her cafés would be known as safe havens where anyone could come and mingle. They'd be a breath of fresh air in a hostile world. She would have a team of people who loved being hospitable, and they would thrive working there.

Wow, how beautiful!

She hurried to write it all down. If this came into fruition, it would definitely be a dream come true.

"Okay, everyone, last question. Let's talk about values. What are the values of your coffee shop?" Ronica asked. "These are not something you choose. They already exist within you. Sometimes the values that drive our behavior are buried so deep and have become so natural, that it makes it hard to describe them and name them. But until you understand them, name them, and communicate them, your values will not spread. What stirs up the passion in you when you think about how your team will interact? How is it different from other coffee shops? Take time to brainstorm and write down all of the behaviors that are important to you. Then later, we will narrow it down to the three most important."

Griffin put his pen in his mouth as a pensive expression crossed his face. The air was thick with critical thinking as people thought about what they truly desired.

"And these are *not* universal values like hard work or punctuality," Ronica added. "Those should go without saying. Your values should not be the bare minimum standard, but they should also not be unachievable."

Claire sat back and looked at the paper in front of her.

"A good way to figure out what your values are is to think about what infuriates you when they are violated," Ronica said.

Claire looked up. She felt like Ronica was speaking directly to her.

The man next to her, Stephen, said, "Like…prioritize repeat customers?"

"Is that a strategy or a value?" Ronica replied. "Strategies are what you do to be successful. Values will not change even if you have to sometimes sacrifice profitability in order to protect them. But maybe it is a value for you if you're not thinking about profitability. Perhaps loyalty is one of your most important values."

Stephen nodded and began writing something down.

"I'll tell you mine to give you a better idea." Everyone perked up and focused on Ronica. "For La Valeur, they are: Prioritize honor, celebrate merit, and experience the excellence of God."

Jennifer stiffened noticeably. Ronica glanced her way. "What's up, Jennifer?"

"I'm sorry, Ronica—something about that just doesn't seem right to me. It seems like you're trying to infiltrate a coffee shop with your religious beliefs," Jennifer said honestly.

"I hear you, Jennifer, but these are my values, not yours. You don't have to agree with it, and I'm not pushing it on people, but I'm being honest that this is what I value," Ronica said patiently.

"Sure, I guess that makes sense." Jennifer looked back down at her paper.

Stephen spoke up again. "So, how is experiencing the excellence of God a value, and not your strategy?"

"Good question, Stephen," Ronica said. "I would say because it permeates all of the behaviors of my staff and myself. Such as making a cup of coffee—if we know that a coffee is anything less than perfect, we'll trash it and start again. Because I'm doing everything as an act of worship." Ronica's face lit up as she continued. "If it was just a strategy, there are some things that are imperfect that I would keep around because people would probably say, 'This is great' anyway, and it can be a waste of money to strive for perfection. But I will not have anything less in my business, and this will never change."

Claire thought about Amber and why the information she had received this morning had infuriated her so much. She felt offended, almost like she was the one who'd been hurt. She thought back to the story she had told Ronica at The Haunt and wrote down on the paper:

1. Inclusiveness

The same light that Ronica glowed with began to find its home in Claire as she stared at the word on her paper. Images and visions began to flood her mind as she considered what *inclusiveness* would look like in her coffee shop.

From the corner of her eye, Ronica caught the look on Claire's face and stopped what she was doing. "Claire?" Claire looked up, blinking a little dazedly. "Would you mind sharing what you wrote down?"

Claire was caught off guard. She stammered, "Yeah…sure." Looking down at her paper, she read it off. "Inclusiveness. My first value is inclusiveness."

Jennifer spoke up, "Is that too general? I mean, doesn't everyone strive for inclusiveness? It's politically correct."

"I'm not saying it to be politically correct," Claire insisted. "I would do anything to make sure that the people in my coffee shop felt like they belonged there." She looked down, her throat starting to get dry as emotions flooded her. "There were some people in my life that made me feel included when I felt like an outsider, and it meant the world to me."

Jennifer nodded, looking slightly surprised at the conviction in Claire's voice.

"Thank you for sharing, Claire," Ronica said. "That's a great example of a value. I know you'll protect that at all costs."

"Absolutely."

Claire turned her attention back to the paper in front of her. She thought about what else would really tick her off if it wasn't executed or worse, if it was violated, and wrote:

2. Consideration

She thought about the year she spent at her parents' house post-college and how difficult the first few months had been. Her sisters quickly learned that one of the most important values she had was "consideration." If she felt considered, she felt loved. To her, a lack of consideration was inconsideration; there was no middle ground.

But how would she consider people more than other coffee shops consider people? Attention to detail and asking great questions.

Did her customer want cow's milk or plant-based milk? Did they know the difference between a cappuccino and a macchiato? When her staff would deliver food, did they need any utensils or sauces? How dark did they like their coffee roasted? Was the music too loud, the temperature too cold? How is their day going? What was new in their lives?

If there were open mic nights, they would be sure to find the customer and deliver their drink right to them. Someone would then go through the crowd and make sure everyone was taken care of.

With her staff, no one would make decisions by thinking only of themselves. They would always be aware of how their actions affected the people around them. Were they thinking of the next person when they did their cleaning duties? Would they willingly pick up and swap shifts? Would they go above and beyond when training new staff members?

She added:

3. Neighborliness

She cared deeply about her coffee shop's neighborhood. She cared about the people who lived there and wanted them to come together. She had even moved into the neighborhood herself after she found the spot for her café. She wanted The Haunt to be a place of companionship and unity.

That meant she and her staff would go out of their way to learn the names of the people in their area, the repeat customers. She would only buy pastries from bakeries in the area, even if she could get a better deal from someone from across town. She would strive to hire people who lived close by.

Maybe she could allow local groups or university clubs to use her space at night when she wasn't hosting open mic nights.

Ronica suddenly clapped her hands. "All right, class is over, everyone. See you tomorrow."

Whoa, was it really already time?

Griffin began putting his things back into his crossbody bag, glancing up at Claire. He leaned over the table. "Hey, Claire, I'm going out to a local open mic night tonight. If you're not busy, would you like to come? Seems like something you'd be into."

Claire's face lit up. Yes, absolutely—but how did he know? The numerous tasks that she had to complete in the morning swirled through her mind, but as quickly as the familiar stress began to roll back in, she stamped it out. She was done living in fear.

"I'd love to!"

Chapter 6: Strategy

Patrons overflowed out of the packed bar onto the sidewalk where casually dressed city-dwellers smoked cigarettes and laughed boisterously in the fresh air, swinging their beer glasses around.

The orange neon signs of the Hungry Falcon welcomed Claire and Griffin as they edged through the crowd inside. With practically every step, Griffin's attention was diverted as he bumped into people he knew.

"Hey, Aaron! What's up, my man?" Griffin locked hands with a man in a flannel shirt, who was sporting a similarly good-looking mustache.

"Hey, Griffin, how's it going!" said a middle-aged woman in cowboy boots and a charcoal tank top. Griffin gave her a warm hug.

They finally made it to the bar, and Griffin looked back at Claire. "Would you like a drink?" he said loudly in an effort to be heard over the general noise.

Claire's eyes were wide with excitement as she digested the scene around her. "Yes, please. Whatever IPA they have on tap."

Claire and Griffin got their drinks and managed to add a couple of seats to a table that was already occupied by, again, some of his friends. Claire was starting to wonder if there was anyone here who didn't know him.

"Do you come here a lot? How do you know so many people?" she bellowed at Griffin.

"I think most people here know each other. This is the spot!" He took a sip of his beer.

"So, it's a lot of the same customers?"

"Yeah, definitely." Griffin looked pleased. "Everyone's from the neighborhood."

One of Griffin's friends looked at her. "And even if they weren't from around here, it wouldn't be long before they knew everyone, too."

"Wow, that's amazing," she said, mostly to herself as she leaned back in her seat.

The woman with the cowboy boots jumped up onto the small stage at the front of the bar and turned on the microphone. "Hey, y'all! Welcome! Are y'all ready for some entertainment?"

The bar erupted in howling and whistling.

Act after act went up to the stage, each one courageous and wonderful.

A woman with a skirt made of colorful patches sang an upbeat folk song that got the whole crowd stomping their feet.

A studious looking young woman with a theatrical demeanor challenged the audience with a poem about wealth inequalities in the city. The crowd nodded along thoughtfully.

Two university students who looked like twins improvised a song by including members of the audience. The audience turned into a roar.

Claire never stopped smiling. Her eyes were aglow like a child's at the first signs of snow.

***

Griffin waited with Claire outside the Hungry Falcon before her taxi showed up. She could see their breath mingling in the chilly air.

"Thank you so much, Griffin, I really needed that." Claire felt lighter and happier than she had in a long time.

"Yeah, no problem, they're a great time, aren't they?" He looked back at the neon sign.

"Yeah, they really are." She said with her hands in her pockets, looking down at the curb. "It's incredible. We need something like that on my side of town."

"Yeah, absolutely." He looked back at her. "I'm fortunate to live here and have found this place. Thanks for reminding me how lucky I am."

"So, how's it been being back?" Claire asked. "Are you enjoying life as a coffee shop owner and watching out for your parents?"

"Good question." Griffin smiled a little sadly and put his hands in his pockets, pondering. "Yeah, it's been something else. I really do love Cuppa. I mean this could really be something to be proud of, to pour all of my energy and creativity into." His face brightened as he thought about the potential. "But I have a really hard time planning for the future. I'm very good at being in the present, but when it comes to the long game, I'm not crazy about it. And that might be the end of me."

"But don't you think this workshop is going to help us with that?" Claire tried to console him.

"Yeah, yeah, I know." He looked down at his shoes for a moment, gathering his thoughts. "I've just been this way for so long, it feels suffocating sometimes to picture myself there for the next five years."

"I see," she said. "Well, why are you doing this, then, Griffin?" He was silent. "You don't have to answer that if you don't want to," she added.

"No, it's cool." He sighed. "It's important for me to remember this."

He stroked his chin and took a deep breath. "Yeah, you know, I grew up in the countryside." He gestured vaguely beyond the Hungry Falcon. "Just outside of the city limits. And it was kind of rough. You think of country folk as being all kind, and I guess they might have been if there wasn't a methamphetamine problem. Coupled with poverty, and a lot of kids growing up seeing their parents wacked out, it was a real mess."

Claire recognized this as a vulnerable moment and gave him her full attention.

"But I never got hooked on that stuff, and that's only because my parents were real saints," Griffin explained. "They also never got into that stuff, but for some reason they still live in that neighborhood."

Griffin, keeping his hands in his pockets, looked toward the sky. "That's why I never came back. We'd talk on the phone a bunch, but for thirteen years, I avoided this place like the plague." He looked at Claire. She returned his gaze, nodding with understanding.

"And then after so many years traveling and mastering the beauty of the moment, I came to the painful realization that I had spent so many years away from my parents—the only people who truly loved me unconditionally and believed in me from day one." His eyes began to get glossy, and he tried to casually look away from Claire.

He paused to gather himself. Claire wanted to remind him that his parents surely would have wanted him to live his life, but instead she said nothing, holding space for him while he processed his feelings.

He looked at her solemn face, and his eyes twinkled. "Oh, stop being so dramatic," he said as he lightly pushed her.

"Oh, come on, let me feel for you." Claire pushed him back.

They laughed as the tension was broken.

"No, it's okay, it's not the full truth," Griffin continued more seriously. "My parents are proud of me, and I'm sure they are more content knowing that I got to see the world."

"That's what I was going to say," Claire said.

He nodded. "So, yeah…why am I doing this? To be close to my parents, but also, I want them to see firsthand who their son has become and what he is capable of. And I'd love to get them out of that hell hole and make sure they're taken care of." His eyes began to light up and his mannerisms became noticeably more animated.

"And it could all be done by creating this exciting and fun oasis in the city. Imagine a place where the staff are never stressed out, even if it means people have to wait a little bit longer." He began to move around, lost in a dream. "A place where people feel like they can leave their stress at the door. A place full of funky art and furniture. A place where the coffee is always good."

The taxi pulled up.

"I can't wait." Claire said with all sincerity. He smiled and they exchanged hugs. Claire hopped off the curb to open the taxi's back door.

"You could make a place like this, Claire!" Griffin called after her, pointing back toward the Hungry Falcon.

A pure grin crossed her face, and she looked back at him, her heart full. "Yeah, I think you're right. Thanks, Griffin."

She got in the taxi and they waved goodbye.

***

"Day three, everyone!" Ronica exclaimed from the front of the class. "All right, get your notebooks out because we are hacking away at these questions. Today, we are switching from questions about your culture to questions about your strategy."

Ronica wiped down the whiteboard, wrote the words *Idea Fatigue* in black marker, and turned to look expectantly toward the class. "Do you guys know what this is?"

No one said anything.

"This is what happens when you are so desperate for something to work that you try *everything*." Ronica spoke with urgency as if she was warning them about the rocks that were coming up ahead. "People are coming into your coffee shop and telling you to change ten different things, and because you don't have a clear strategy, you try a little of this and a little of that. But you are not able to give any of the ideas the passion and attention they need to execute them well.

"It would be like a chef opening the refrigerator and grabbing a little of everything and throwing it into a casserole. There's no plan or vision for the dish. Anybody want that for dinner? That is how your regulars feel. Your customers from yesterday are confused about the most recent idea you're trying today.

"And what's worse is that every decision is a burden for you. After a while, even simple decisions wear you out. It's because you do not have a guiding strategy to align your decisions with."

Ronica gave the audience a knowing look. "I'm guessing some of you understand what I'm talking about."

The nods around the room showed that everyone knew all too well what she was talking about.

"What you do want is a clear strategy," Ronica told them. "Once you have a clear strategy, you will be able to make decisions almost effortlessly. Question number four is: *Who are you serving?* I experienced the most idea fatigue when I was trying strategies that would be good for customers in a different neighborhood but not the customers in my location."

Ronica turned toward the whiteboard and began writing down questions:

What do they like?
What do they do?

What do they value?
How do they think?
What are their biggest challenges?

Griffin sat up straight. "Why not just follow your gut and serve them that way?"

"Not all of us are as in tune with the universe as you are," Jennifer joked.

"I'm just saying, do whatever works for you," Griffin retorted. "Humans aren't that complicated."

Ronica turned away from the whiteboard. "I understand where you're coming from, Griffin, and you make a good point. However, it's important that you ask whether or not your target audience is like you. Do the people that come to your coffee shop think like you do? If you are essentially in the same demographic and psychographic as them, your intuition will serve you well. But you have to be honest with yourself and ask if your customers like what you like. If you are different than your target customer, then your intuition will lead you astray."

"Hmm," Griffin looked down at his paper and became consumed by his thoughts.

Ronica continued writing on the board:

How would you define them?
Mostly male/female?
What's the age group?

"These are demographics," she said. "But it is even more important to think about psychographics like these."

What issues are they concerned about?
What are their values?
What brands do they like and why?
How important are environmental issues?
What social issues are they thinking about?

Ronica turned back toward the class. "You have to be as specific as possible. How do your customers view the world? Why do they go to coffee shops? What are their values?"

Claire thought about it. She had quite a mix going on in her shop. She had young moms and young professionals, college students, and businesspeople. But if pressed, she'd say that the young professionals and college students made up the majority.

So, forward-thinking people who needed a place to meet, study, and work. It was also likely that they were on the go pretty often. Most of them were probably thirty-five and younger, and she would say middle-class.

Brands that they liked were probably not cheap but not expensive either, just expensive enough to be ethical. They liked good coffee but at a reasonable price. Usually, they weren't too hung up on the perfection of the coffee, but they cared about environmental and social issues.

"Question number five," proclaimed Ronica. "*What does your customer want most and what problem are you solving for them?* Start with the greatest need and then go to maybe three or four smaller needs.

"It is helpful here to think in terms of priority. Everyone would say that speed of service, quality of product, customer experience, coffee shop environment, and price are all important. But each type of customer has a different order of importance. And you won't be able to prioritize everything. You must hone in on what your specific target customer wants most and deliver that better and more consistently than your competitors.

"Think about things like…"

She went back to the whiteboard:

Is this a health-conscious area?
Do people just want some caffeine in their day?
Is it a working-class neighborhood and people need cheap, decent coffee?
Is it a good place for a business meeting?

Claire tapped her pencil lightly on the table as she mulled the questions over. The clarity was making her both anxious and hopeful as she realized that she really had been trying to prioritize everything. It made sense why no one was wowed by any of her mediocre efforts.

What was the greatest problem that she was solving? What did her customers want most? Why were they coming to her shop? What need was she fulfilling?

She thought about the neighborhood that she was in and how her coffee shop fit into that. The coffee shop closest to her was called "Momo," and it had a modern, industrial design. It was very open and spacious, minimalist furniture, no couches, all small tables and chairs. Momo was the chic coffee shop, with more forward-thinking, more expensive coffee.

The other coffee shop in the neighborhood was a coffee drive-thru, which obviously served the on-the-go need.

She was the casual hang. That was it! She was the casual coffee shop, with living room furniture, some bigger tables and small tables. She was the cozy place where people could lounge, or work, or meet their friends and feel relaxed without spending too much money.

Over the past six months, she had received several suggestions from customers who also frequented Momo's who had suggested a more minimalist design. Claire had tried to accommodate them by removing some of the decorations and furniture that were the character of her café. In doing so, she had disappointed other customers who came for the welcoming atmosphere.

Although she realized her blunder, she still felt hopeful because it was all starting to make sense. Different people have different needs. Now that she knew who she was serving and what made her shop unique, she would not experience so much whiplash and idea fatigue.

Claire smiled to herself. That pleased her.

"Moving on, folks, question number six: *What makes your café special?* There's lots of competition out there, and even if you think you're special, does your customer think you're special? Do you actually stand out? I will go across town to my favorite coffee shop because it hits everything I need it to. Are you that coffee shop for someone? The most dangerous thing you can do is be safe."

Some of the glow began to fade as Claire was confronted with the fact that her café was, frankly, mediocre. Ronica was right. Claire could list the reasons she thought The Haunt was unique, but what would her customers say? Was being the casual hang in the neighborhood enough? Probably not.

What made her special?

Right now, maybe nothing. There were probably lots of coffee shops in the city with a cozy, casual environment. She was definitely being safe.

Okay, so what could she do to make her coffee shop special?

Ronica began making rounds around the table, stopping to talk to each of the thoughtful coffee shop owners.

Claire knew that her customers were young professionals and college students. She knew that they weren't looking for the most expensive coffee and that they needed somewhere casual to hang out and work. But what could she do to keep them there and draw more people in?

Maybe her draw wasn't even the daytime. She thought about when she'd been a college student; as long as the place was comfortable, had open seats, was close by and served decent coffee, she would be there.

Maybe her draw was the nighttime when she would host open mic nights. And out of all the open mic nights in town, how would she get people to come to hers? How did coffee shops or bars become known for their open mic nights? It needed to be a place where performers felt comfortable and confident. Where they would want to perform. She would surely need great marketing to get the word out. Somehow, she hoped she'd be able to advertise at the university.

What would make her special? Amazing open mic nights. That's where her focus needed to be.

Ronica stopped at Claire.

"Hey, Claire, will you share what you wrote for what makes your coffee shop special?" Ronica said. "Let's make sure it's solid."

"Oh yeah, no problem," Claire said. "I wrote down, *open mic nights*."

Ronica nodded slowly. "So, I didn't want to say this to you before, but open mic nights truly can only work under certain conditions," she said honestly. "For instance, your rent has to be low enough that you can afford to have people standing around."

Claire thought about this for a moment. "I'd say I'm paying an average amount each month."

Ronica continued, "At least The Haunt isn't in the middle of the city. I can imagine it's a little cheaper where you are. But still, I imagine you'll have to raise your coffee prices or have an item that both sells well and has a high margin on those nights."

Claire nodded thoughtfully.

"Just keep it in mind, Claire. We'll get more into finances later." Ronica gave Claire a pat on the shoulder and continued on.

Claire did not want to see her dreams dashed. She was determined to make this work no matter the cost.

Chapter 7: Tactics

After Grace had given sixth-grade Claire the confidence she needed to enjoy middle school, Claire had decided to join theater.

On the stage, she was allowed to be untamed and eccentric, without any social backlash. The more uninhibited, the better in the theater.

One time, she played as Anne Boleyn's decapitated head. Her head sat on top of a table, made possible by a hole cut in the middle, while the rest of her body was hidden underneath by a long tablecloth. She had more lines than one might expect from a decapitated head, and the audience ate it up.

In the spring of that year, she sang as a citizen of Emerald City in *The Wizard of Oz*. That's when Claire found out that she loved to sing.

But she'd never forget eighth grade when she was chosen for the lead role in Shakespeare's *Antony and Cleopatra*. After getting the news, she'd floated all the way to the bus after school and all the way home.

When opening night came, she remembered staring at herself in the dressing room mirror. Her eyes stared back in bold, dark eyeliner, and the gold of an Egyptian queen dripped off her shoulders. The girl staring back at her was fearless.

She could hardly remember the timid girl who entered middle school, alone and afraid. *This* was who Claire Wallace was always meant to be.

Images ran through her head…the silent crowd in rows of red plush seats. The blast of light that flooded the stage. All the eyes on her as she escaped into ancient Egypt and took them with her. The final bow, the flowers at her feet, the cheering and applause. Her smile that could have warmed a stadium.

Fifteen minutes after she was supposed to get up, Claire was still lying in her bed, staring at the ceiling while the memories played through her mind.

She hadn't continued with theater after high school, but it had served its purpose in her life. Theater was the first time she truly felt like she mattered among her peers. It was the first time she realized she had something to give to the world around her. It was the first time she had a community, a place where she belonged.

Claire pulled herself out of bed and toward the bathroom.

This was where her love of open mics came from. There was this beautiful exchange that happened between the audience and performer. The audience received the gift of the performer's talent and vulnerability, and the performer got to drink in their acceptance and appreciation.

Claire stopped in front of the mirror and stared at her reflection as a realization came to her mind. She hadn't allowed herself to truly commit to open mic nights.

Some of her former co-workers had become regulars at The Haunt. They were well intentioned and wanted to support her, but they had made some comments trivializing open mic nights, and that had put a dent in her spirit.

But now she saw that if this was going to be a core part of her strategy, she couldn't just have open mic nights for the people who already enjoyed them; she had to make them so amazing that the people who thought they didn't enjoy them wanted to go as well.

Claire finished getting ready. With a granola bar and coffee in her hand, she ran out the door.

***

Claire walked into Ronica's workshop with a small coffee stain on her blouse. Whatever; if there was anywhere in the world that she wouldn't be judged for a coffee stain, it had to be here.

"Good morning!" she said to the room. She found her seat next to Jennifer, who acknowledged her with a casual head nod and got back to the email she was answering on her phone.

Ronica had become more and more casual as time went on and was now wearing a La Valeur sweatshirt and some jeans. Her demeanor was also casual as she treated everyone like good pals, yet she commanded the respect of the room.

It was crazy that it had only been four days, but Claire also felt noticeably more comfortable with the people in the room.

"Hey, everyone. Welcome," Ronica said. "Day four already! We're finishing the rest of the questions today. Tomorrow will be our last day together before the real fun begins." Her smile looked almost mischievous. "All right, are you all ready to answer some questions?"

Confident nods rippled around the room.

"Now, we are switching over to questions about your tactics. Beginning with question number seven: *What are the key things you need to measure to make sure your coffee shop will be successful?*"

She began writing on the whiteboard.

> *Average Ticket Value*
> *Average Daily Tickets*
> *Number of New Customers*
> *Number of New Customers That Have Visited 5x*
> *Customer Frequency*
> *Customer Satisfaction*

"Every coffee shop should be measuring these aspects of their business," Ronica said. "But where you'll differ is when you measure the aspects of your coffee shop that make you unique. Once you find that thing that your customers love, you need to protect and fortify that. Which means you need to keep track of it."

Claire thought about this. How would she measure open mic nights? She began making a list on her paper.

1. How many people are showing up for open mic nights?
2. How many performers are signing up?
3. What are our average sales during open mic nights?
4. How many people are returning?

"Question number eight," Ronica continued. "*What is the most important problem that must be solved within the next six months?* In a busy business, with hundreds of tasks to be taken care of every day, it's usually the short-term, most urgent problems that receive the most attention. But these are not necessarily the most important tasks. Even though they are urgent, they might not be what keeps you open in six months.

"That's why it's important to pick one long-term problem that must be taken care of if the café is going to be successful. You should think of this problem as, 'If this problem is not solved, then nothing else matters.' This should be a rally cry for your staff, and if it is done well, it will align all of your employees."

Claire looked over at Griffin. "Long-term plans, huh?" she teased. "I'm here if you need moral support."

Griffin smiled and rolled his eyes.

Well, there was no doubt that she needed to get these open mic nights off the ground. What would a successful open mic night look like to her?

She had to plan an open mic night that would set the bar for the following open mic nights.

Well, in six months she should be able to host an open mic night with at least five different performers in a room at least half full, with everyone brandishing a drink or a pastry. That was achievable.

But how would she achieve the feeling that she was going for? Her true goal was for people to feel connected, included, and cool.

Maybe if she had at least one polished performer to kick things off and build the right energy. Perhaps they could perform again if there was a lull in the evening…

"Question number nine," Ronica went on. "*Who will do what to make sure this goal is achieved?*"

Claire scribbled out a list that included her two baristas and manager, Frankie.

Me: Put together the details/concept, host
Violet: Work the bar that night, work the room
Amber: Pass out fliers, find the equipment
Frankie: Create marketing plan and materials

"And lastly!" exclaimed Ronica. "Question number ten: *How and when will you follow up on the progress of these questions we went over today?* Let me tell you right now—if you do not follow up with your team on these things every single week, people will get busy and they will forget. That's just how people are. They forget, they get caught up, they get distracted."

Okay, easy enough—a little team meeting every week. Claire would just have to find a day that worked for Violet, Amber, and Frankie, and she'd have to stay on top of it. No more getting lost in her own sea of tasks and exhaustion.

Ronica continued speaking. "I used to think that the goal of running a coffee shop was to work really hard, all the time. That is not your goal. Your goal is to give yourself permission to invest time into the things that really matter. Are your actions lining up with what you've said are the most important aspects of your business?"

It was true that for at least a year, Claire's actions had not represented her deepest motivations. It was all surface-level stuff that she'd done to try and stay afloat.

But that was all going to change.

Chapter 8: Introduction to Systems

It was the last day of the workshop, and Claire was overflowing with optimism. The hope that Ronica had planted had bloomed into a vision of what her coffee shop could become. Adrenaline coursed through her as she anticipated the next six months. She forced herself to eat a bite of her granola bar and set it down. She felt as if she had been surviving off dreams and excitement the past forty-eight hours.

She surveyed the room, wondering how her fellow coffee shop owners were faring.

Jennifer was fidgeting with her pen and staring hard at her notepad. Claire could almost see the reflection of Jennifer's to-do list in her glasses.

Griffin walked in the room, clutching his messenger bag, a confident grin on his face. Claire couldn't put her finger on it, but he seemed more grounded, more certain of his ability to exist in this world as a coffee shop owner.

Stephen, wearing his regulation khakis, was sitting to her right. He seemed like the most normal one here, and yet Claire still felt like she was missing something about him. He was clearly smart, and he engaged well with the class…but only as long as it didn't get too personal. He liked talking about concepts, but he didn't like talking about concepts as they related to his business. He liked talking about the personal freedom that a thriving business could provide, but he was vague when it came to talking about the freedom he himself was or wasn't experiencing.

And finally, there was Ronica, who had been the guide that Claire needed in a dark season. Claire smiled at her with warm admiration as Ronica was putting together all her papers and getting ready to start the workshop.

She got up, catching's Claire look and returning the smile. "All right, everyone. We are here, on the last day of the workshop." She looked around the room, making eye contact with each person sitting in the familiar conference area.

"You guys came here to gain clarity on your coffee shop, to refocus on your strategy, and now it's time to move forward." Ronica beamed. "The work has just begun. Now you guys are going to go back to your team. All the answers that you came up with here, you need to share that with your employees." Ronica paused and her face grew serious. "And unfortunately, if your employees aren't going to fully support you in this, you're going to have to find people who will. That might be the first step for a lot of you."

Claire thought about her team and wondered what that was going to look like for her. She wondered about Amber—could she inspire her to get on board?

"Perhaps many of you hired people out of desperation or because they were really great at their job, but if they're not going to support your why and your values, and if they don't want to get your coffee shop to that ten-year goal, then it's better to let them go."

The tone of Ronica's voice told them that this was not something they could compromise on. "Allow them to find a place that better suits them," she said.

Ronica turned toward the whiteboard and picked up a marker. "Make sure you're writing these steps down. After you talk to your team, you're going to begin aligning your coffee shop with your culture and strategy. Here are some good questions to check your cultural alignment."

She began writing:

- What staff members embody our culture?
- What team members consistently violate our values?
- Does my marketing communicate my mission?
- Are we hiring the right people?

"And here are some good questions to check your strategic alignment," she added.

- *Do the products we're serving fit with our strategy?*
- *Does the way we're marketing fit with strategy?*
- *Does our operation align with our strategy?*

Ronica looked back at the class. "When I went back to La Valeur after taking a workshop like this, I realized that there were a lot of aspects of my business that were way off from what I was truly going for. On top of that, the parts of my strategy that I *was* implementing, I was not executing in a way that was 'all in.' In order for a strategy to do its job, it has to be implemented in such a way that it rises above the noise, and people not only notice it, but they start talking about it.

"One example is that I was hiring people who had barista experience, but they were willing to take shortcuts and didn't care about excellence. One of my strategies: hire people who have a record of executing their work with integrity. Not many coffee shop owners contact references. I do.

"And then I went further—I took excellence to a radical extreme. With every pour-over, we pour a small portion of it into a separate glass and the barista tastes it. If it doesn't taste excellent, we dump the pour-over out and do it again. We set stringent QC measures on all of our products, and we share them with our customers. Our croissants are served at exactly 8:08 every morning and are only available until 8:38 because they are only at their best for thirty minutes. I donated all of my old cups to Goodwill, and I purchased all new coffee cups that our customers can't stop talking about."

Ronica paused, making eye contact with everyone in the room.

"Let me put it this way: I had to take my strategy of excellence from something that *I* could see in the business to such an extreme that busy people can't help but notice it, experience it, and be moved by it."

She turned back toward the whiteboard. "All right, after you align your coffee shop with your strategy, you're going to look at systems."

She wrote on the board:

- *Focused systemization*
- *Restrained systemization*

"Systems are like lines on the road. We all need a certain amount of restraint to keep us focused. This is focused systemization. What you're trying to do is make systems for the things that are causing pain in your business. Are you constantly getting customers' orders wrong? Are you always running out of products? Create a system to solve that problem."

Griffin's eyes darted around the room and he opened his mouth, obviously antsy. "Okay, I can understand that, but when are systems too much? How do you balance between systems easing your pain versus cramping your style?"

Ronica nodded. "The worst mistake you can make with systems is what we call 'unrestrained systemization.' I've seen this many times where people take systems too far and decide to make a system for everything because they see how helpful they are.

"This is what happens: people have pain in an area, and they create a system for that problem. Then they feel the relief from solving that problem. Suddenly they're in love with systems and the value that they bring. They start implementing systems for everything. Then, their coffee shop gets bogged down by over-systematizing. As a result, their staff disregard both the bad *and* the good systems.

"With focused systemization, you take a minimalist or essentialist approach to systems by using systems to fix only what is broken or breaking and by creating the simplest system possible.

"Once the systems are causing you more pain than the actual problem, stop. This is 'restrained systemization.'"

Griffin seemed to be satisfied with that, and he relaxed visibly.

Jennifer had been shifting uneasily in her seat. Now she blurted out, "Okay, but you're going to repeat this information to us over the next six months, right? I don't know if I'm going to be able to remember all of this and successfully implement all of it." She sounded slightly frantic and looked overwhelmed.

There was compassion in Ronica's voice when she answered. "You're going to have a million questions once you get started. There's no doubt about it. But not only will you have me to walk you through it, but you'll have each other. We will check in with each other regularly as we tackle each step of the process, one at a time, *together*."

Jennifer digested with a few slow nods. "Okay, that sounds good," she said.

Stephen chimed in. "Is that when you're going to give us specifics about what works and what doesn't work in coffee shops? Like, do loyalty programs work? What drinks sell the best in this region? Is it a good idea to incorporate a drive-thru? Et cetera."

Claire jumped in. "I think that depends on your strategy and what you're trying to do. From what I understand, there is no right or wrong."

Stephen looked slightly frustrated. Looking at Ronica, he said, "There's really not a 'what works best and what doesn't work?'"

Ronica nodded. "That's right. It truly depends on the strategy you decide on based on who you are serving."

Stephen's frown deepened.

Claire empathized with him. "Stephen, are you having a hard time feeling confident about making those decisions?" she asked.

Stephen looked down and around at the classroom, leaning back in his chair with a pen in one of his hands. "No, no, not necessarily."

Claire wasn't convinced, but she nodded and let it go.

"Well, before we end, does anyone want to share how they're feeling right now about it all?" Ronica asked. "Any differences from the beginning to the end of the workshop? Anyone feeling optimistic or maybe nervous? It's okay to be honest about that."

The class was silent for a moment, then Griffin began. "Thanks for asking, Ronica." He straightened up in his chair and looked around at everyone.

"I'm somewhere in between. I'm walking into unknown territory where the stakes are pretty high, so that makes me slightly uncomfortable. But the clarity is really helpful and it's nice to truly understand what Cuppa is about. I'm feeling confident overall. I believe this is going to work out in the end."

Ronica's face glowed with pride. "That's great, Griffin. I really believe you can do it. Anyone else?"

"I'm definitely feeling overwhelmed," Jennifer confessed. She crossed her legs and arms and looked down at whatever was written on the notepad in front of her. "But I guess being overwhelmed with the right information and having direction is better than being overwhelmed and not knowing what to do." She smirked as she thought about something. "I mean, I'm really good at coffee. And I say that with humility as someone who has invested endless hours into understanding it. But I'm not great with business."

Ronica nodded understandingly. "Coffee seems to be one of those industries where it's easy to forget about the business part. You're not alone in that. And if you take each step one at a time, you'll be a coffee *and* business expert in no time."

Jennifer breathed out, "Yes, that's all I can do, right?"

Stephen was absently moving his pen around in his hand next to Claire. She looked over at him and then back at Ronica.

"It's funny," she began. "I thought that by working a corporate job in a huge company for three years, that I would understand business. But I don't think I really understood anything." She laughed. "It's so different starting your own business. I was beginning to think the business world wasn't for me. But now, I feel like I can really make something happen with The Haunt."

Claire beamed at Ronica who gave her a little wink.

"It's going to be great, I can see it now," Ronica replied. "And listen, everyone." She looked around the room. "Your business isn't going to be perfect in six months. This will take time. But if before you were wandering in circles around a dark forest, you will end this journey walking down the right path, going in the right direction."

People began collecting their things, ready to leave, but Ronica stopped them.

"I know you guys are ready to get going, but let's talk about one more thing before I release you. This will be your task for tomorrow."

The room stilled in anticipation.

"We're going to start with systematizing your finances." Ronica began handing out a stack of papers.

Jennifer looked decidedly unenthused. Griffin leaned over the table toward her. "Come on, Jennifer, if anyone is good with finances, it must be you," he whispered, smiling.

"It's not that I'm not *good* at them," she replied. "It's that I don't *like* them."

Griffin sat back in his chair. "Touché."

Ronica overheard Jennifer's remark. "To be honest, I've rarely heard people say that they are passionate about finances. A lot of people struggle with them."

Some of Claire's giddy optimism faded. *Finances.* This was the part of her business that was the most difficult for her to face. It was like going to the dentist; she avoided it because she always received bad news.

But Ronica continued, "Your finances will be the first—and most important—area of your business that you will systematize."

Claire looked down at the paper Ronica had put in front of her and saw that it was a spreadsheet with different financial terms labeled on it.

"It's almost like having an unused room where random things are thrown into and hid," Ronica explained. "Having finances that are not in order creates a place where problems can hide. If you don't have your finances organized, it's going to be hard to organize anything else."

Stephen raised his hand.

"Yes, Stephen?" Ronica said.

"When we're talking about finances, are we talking about keeping up on your bookkeeping?" he asked.

"Good question," she said. "That is important, especially when you're breaking even or not doing well, but that's not the first priority."

She turned toward the board and drew a coffee cup.

"You need to know the basic numbers of your business." She began writing numbers. "How much are you selling a cup of coffee for and how much does it cost to make that cup of coffee? The ingredients should be costing you 25 to 30 percent of what the product costs."

She continued writing. "And what are your monthly expenses? After you know that, then you can work backwards and figure out how many customers you need to walk in each day to break even, and then to be profitable. Look forward as you plan. This will be the basis for all future planning. Next, you'll need to have your financial records available electronically so that you can compare your predictions to your results. You'll be able to use these numbers to predict outcomes in your business."

She turned back around. "And that's how you know you're done with systemization—when you can predict your financial performance in advance." She smiled at the class.

Wow, that actually wasn't as difficult as Claire was expecting. She wrote down some notes and then raised her hand.

"Yes, Claire?"

"So, what goes wrong here?" she asked. "Why are finances such a beast?"

Ronica smiled as the class chuckled. "I think there's a couple reasons. One is that people are often surprised by which products are making money and which aren't. There are also a lot of miscellaneous expenses to be aware of. You have to be very thorough about understanding each number of your business."

She continued with a sigh. "And then of course there's the shame around it. People don't want to do their bookkeeping when things are going great, let alone when things are going badly. But it's never wise to ignore them. I thought things were going great but because I wasn't keeping up with my numbers, it took a while for me to realize that I wasn't doing well at all. We were so busy, and we were able to pay most of our bills, so I assumed we were more profitable than we were. What I didn't realize was that the amount I owed to our suppliers and credit card companies was consistently creeping up. I was actually digging a financial hole. When I finally did make time to catch up on our books, it was very discouraging. It felt unfair to work so hard but not make enough money to get ahead."

Claire nodded as she studied the spreadsheet. She knew all too well what that shame felt like.

"The last reason people don't like finances is that they believe they're not good at it," Ronica said. "Or that they can't be good at it. The fact is that anyone can be good at it with practice. And anything can be enjoyable if you are good at it. You will meet very few successful businesspeople who don't like accounting. Think of accounting as the score to the game—if you're winning, keeping score is fun." Ronica looked around the room. "Would anyone be willing to share their financial situation?"

Griffin shrugged. "Yeah, I don't mind, because to be honest I don't really know how I'm doing. I have admittedly been very laissez faire about everything. It seems to have worked for me in the past. But perhaps that's not the case for business. But after hearing your story, I should probably pay more attention no matter what appears to be happening."

Ronica smiled. "Yes, I would definitely recommend that. Thank you for sharing, Griffin."

Jennifer groaned softly. "Uh, yeah. It hasn't been easy for me to be sustainable. I love creating new inventions and being innovative with coffee, but I haven't made my finances a priority." She looked around the room, disheartened. "With all the recent success at Obsidian, I should have been making more money, but I'm barely breaking even right now. I need to change, but I don't want to sacrifice our position as the innovators and thought leaders of our industry."

Ronica nodded. "I can understand that," she said. "It's possible you'll need to make some sacrifices, but I'm sure there's a balance where you can do both. I don't want you to lose that innovation."

Jennifer made eye contact with Ronica and then slumped back into her chair, thinking to herself.

"All right, everyone," Ronica said. "Fill out those spreadsheets tomorrow and stay on top of the Facebook group. That's where we'll talk and where you'll receive further instructions over the next six months. It's been a pleasure, and I look forward to seeing what you all accomplish."

Claire was busy trying to squish her notebook into her purse when she saw Stephen placing the last item into his backpack as he got up to go.

"Hey, Stephen!" Claire didn't know what she was about to say but something compelled her to stop him.

He looked up, clearly surprised, but he nodded pleasantly. "What's up?"

She shrugged. "I guess I just wanted to check in on you. Are you ready for these next six months?" She made her voice as upbeat as possible to hide her doubt.

He thought about it for a moment, slightly pursing his lips. "Yeah, I think so. It should be chill."

She hesitated, then spoke her mind. "Forgive me for being blunt. Maybe I'm just completely misreading you, but are you really in this?"

As soon as the words were out, she wondered if she'd overstepped. *Why Claire? Why was that necessary? Who are you to say something like that?*

Stephen looked caught off guard, but he handled it with ease. And then he gave her an answer she was not expecting. "I'm trying to be."

Claire looked him straight in the eyes. "What do you truly want, Stephen?"

"Everything," he said with a smile. "I want everything. I want to travel. I want to create more businesses. I want to be mentored. Perhaps create a non-profit. I want to see the world. Man, so many ideas."

Claire smiled with him. "I believe in that. I hope you can follow your heart."

"Thanks, Claire, I appreciate it."

She patted him on the shoulder and walked out the door.

Part III
Systems

Chapter 9: Finances

The afternoon sun poured into Claire's bedroom making her squint as she looked out the window. A sudden gust swept through the street and sent the fallen leaves dancing through the air. It was a beautiful day, and there was no telling how many more would be like it with winter approaching in a month or two.

The bright red tree across the street seemed to call her name, and the romantic in her pushed her out the door and down the stairs.

Outside, she stopped to take a deep breath of the fresh autumn air. It was just what she needed to clear her mind.

She had spent all morning and early afternoon on her finances, looking up the cost of everything from milk to cinnamon and calculating how much of each ingredient was needed to make every product until it exhausted her. Then she would lie on her floor and groan, do some stretching, and get back at it.

Ronica was right: there were definitely some expenses that had hidden themselves in the shadows of her negligence.

Some of the products that she'd thought were moneymakers were actually pretty expensive when she broke down the cost of their ingredients. On the flip side, she was surprised to see certain products making her more money than she would have guessed.

And then there was the thing that Ronica had talked about when it came to open mic nights being profitable. Her rent wasn't as expensive as other locations, but she was going to have to raise the prices of some of her products to afford people standing around.

She also thought about selling something specific on those nights that would be a crowd pleaser and could make up for the lost income.

Claire walked along the sidewalk, her eyes wide-open, drinking in all the beauty. She smiled at a dignified older woman who was walking her dalmatian. She looked over to her right and glanced at the familiar ice cream shop across the way. She thought about how it must be tough for ice cream businesses during the colder months. Perhaps if they had something warm to go with it—

Wait a second.

What if that warm thing was...espresso? In doing her finances, she had discovered that her affogatos, the famous drink that combines espresso with ice cream, had one of the highest margins at her shop.

Claire continued walking, ruminating on this fact. What if she made flavored affogatos and got a little crazy with them? But only on open mic nights. She could do mocha affogatos or caramel affogatos.

Claire walked back to her apartment congratulating herself on what a genius she was. She could surely mark those up as well and treat them as a dessert. She was sure that people would pay for them.

Claire walked into her apartment and sat back down at her desk in her bedroom. She studied the numbers and began making some calculations.

It wasn't long before Claire's eyes once again caught the final number circled in red at the bottom of her spreadsheet. Her hope popped like a balloon.

She put aside her calculations and stared at that number. Before going on her walk, Claire had found out that she was making even less money than she'd thought. Not a lot less, but enough to make her discouraged.

Anxiety rose in her chest and began to make its way through the rest of her body, as debilitating thoughts soaked into her mind. The fear was crippling.

How would her dad take it? He was an investor, and he knew that sometimes investors lost money, that's just how it was. But that didn't mean he'd be nice about it.

If she thought he was demeaning now, how would he act if she was the daughter who had cost him thousands of dollars? Even after all these years, she still wanted to make her father proud. But if this didn't work out, she doubted she'd ever succeed.

Claire put her head down on her papers and clenched her eyes shut. She wanted to be done with this. She stayed there for a couple minutes before lifting her head back up. She took a deep breath and rubbed her face.

"One step at a time, Claire," she murmured. "It's going to work out."

She continued making her calculations for open mic night and doing the work of figuring out how many people had to walk in the door in order for her to be profitable.

She began getting rid of items that were sucking the money out of the business and raised prices where she could.

She simplified her ingredient list and double-checked her fixed expenses every month.

Just then the screen of her phone lit up with a notification from the Coffee Shop Management Group.

Ronica was asking for people to share their experiences working on the spreadsheet.

A comment from Griffin popped up immediately. "This is terrible, anyone want to grab a beer after this?"

Claire chuckled. "Count me in!" she typed back.

Claire typed out her affogato idea and her findings for the day.

Then Jennifer commented on the post. "I might have been more vigilant about this a long time ago if I had known that it was this simple. I'm definitely not where I want to be financially, but I'm feeling hopeful and seeing that I can be smarter about this without sacrificing what I love about Obsidian."

Griffin's response was immediate. "Right on, Jennifer! Go for it!"

Claire's heart went out to Griffin thinking about what he might be going through right now if Cuppa wasn't doing well. Was he thinking about his parents and feeling discouraged?

***

Low beats were playing on the speaker in Griffin's office while he absently doodled on the spreadsheet before him. As he was finishing the cape of his newly drawn superhero, he suddenly realized that he was doing it again.

Griffin blew out a breath of air in frustration. Dropping his pen, he leaned back in his chair with his hands behind his head, surrendering to his utterly bored state-of-mind.

It actually hadn't been *that* bad. He was pleasantly surprised to find that there were many aspects of his business that were going well. But he was also losing money and hadn't even realized it.

He knew that if he wanted to make something out of Cuppa, he was going to have to push through the discomfort of his finances and stay on top of them. Consistently. It seemed so oppressive to him, to have to deal with minute details like this forever.

But that was what he signed up for when he started a business.

Griffin looked over at his desk. The pictures standing on the wooden surface stared back as if they were trying to remind him of something.

One was a picture of himself with his parents when he had first come back to the city a year ago. He was crouching between them as they sat at the familiar kitchen table that he had eaten meals at throughout his childhood years.

In their old age, the veins popped from their hands and his mother's hair was noticeably thinner. But their smiles were fresh and glowed with pride as they posed with their son.

Griffin sat up and put his elbows on the desk.

The picture right next to it was of nineteen-year-old Griffin standing in front of the Pantheon in Greece. It was the first place he had ever traveled to outside of the United States and was perhaps still one of the most magical sites he'd ever seen.

Griffin's eighteenth Christmas landed smack dab in the middle of perhaps the darkest winter of his life. He had graduated from high school the summer before and he had big dreams for his life.

Neither he nor his family had any money; in fact, they were used to taking the occasional cold shower when they had to choose between food or the gas bill. But that ultimately wasn't what stopped him from leaving right after he graduated.

Griffin had stayed in that wretched neighborhood because his closest friend, Paulie, had lost his mother that summer to a drug overdose.

It didn't feel right for Griffin to take off in the middle of that, so he decided to stay until affairs had been settled with Paulie's younger siblings and with Paulie himself, who had taken the loss especially hard.

And even after all of that, even though death hung in the air, most of his friends were still hooked on methamphetamines. It could have been him if his parents hadn't rallied around him the way they did when they'd first found out he was using.

He had tried to save his friends, but nothing worked. His heart had sunk to new levels of defeat and the darkness seemed to overwhelm him.

It was particularly cold in their household that Christmas. His sister, who lived down the block with her two kids, had come over with her husband.

Griffin watched as the kids opened their presents. He'd tried to get himself into the holiday spirit and forced a smile onto his face, but it was hollow. His parents cheerfully handed their grandchildren stockings with their names stitched onto the red sleeves.

While the kids were exclaiming over their stockings, Griffin's sister came and sat down next to him.

"Are you all right, Griffin?" she asked softly.

He looked over at her and smirked. "How could you tell?"

"Because you usually have more light in those eyes." She said it kindly, but it was clear she was concerned.

Griffin crossed his arms in front of him and leaned back in his chair. "Yeah, I'm okay. I'm just trying to…hold onto some hope."

His sister nodded like she understood all too well. "Why don't you allow yourself to focus on the good things for one day?"

He smiled at her. "Yeah, you're right. I'm sorry."

Just then Griffin's mom walked up behind him and handed him a card. She sat back down next to Griffin's dad, and suddenly the entire atmosphere of the room changed.

Griffin's sister and brother-in-law and even the kids were staring at him in anticipation.

Griffin looked around suspiciously. "What's going on here?"

No one said anything and Griffin looked at the card in his hand.

"It's for you, bud, go on and open it." His dad grinned.

"All right…" Griffin, confused, opened the card.

He pulled out what looked like a ticket and his eyes jumped around the paper, putting together all of the information on it, trying to understand what was happening here.

His heart began to race.

He registered the words, "Delta," "Athens, Greece," and a flight number. And a date: January 25.

He looked up in shock. "Is this a flight to Greece?"

Tears began to fall down his mom's face, and his sister sniffed. Griffin's father tried to hide his own emotions and tapped his foot restlessly.

"How could you guys afford this?" Griffin asked in disbelief.

His sister spoke up. "Mom's been saving up." Griffin's mom was nodding her head and patting her eyes with a tissue. His sister continued with her warm smile. "We're trying to get you out of here."

"You don't belong here, Griffin," said his father as he rested his hand on Griffin's knee. "Notice that's a one-way ticket, son. Get out there."

Griffin came out of the memory and stared at the picture on his desk.

He had to do it for them.

He looked back over at the spreadsheet. He just needed to take it one item at a time. Once he'd figured out his monthly expenses and how much everything was costing him, then he'd be able to work backward to see how many customers he needed.

He could do this.

Chapter 10: Hiring

The clatter of beans rang through the air and the smell of caramel wafted through the door as Claire walked into The Haunt.

Violet's back was to her as she cleaned some equipment at the sink, while Amber was busy working on a drink behind the bar.

"Macchiato for Paul!" Amber yelled out as she placed the drink on the bar. A young man stepped forward in a tweed suit and picked up the drink.

"Thank you," he said and walked out the door past Claire.

It was nice to be here today, although she was nervous to explain to her staff what she had been up to.

"Hey, Amber." Claire approached the bar.

Amber turned to face Claire. "Oh, hey, Claire," she said, her voice carefully neutral.

"Hi, Claire!" Violet called over her shoulder from the sink, her hands dripping in suds.

"Hi, Violet." Claire smiled. "Are you guys ready to meet?" It was the afternoon lull and Claire figured this shouldn't take too long.

Frankie came out from the back hearing the familiar ring of his boss's voice, carrying freshly printed papers in his hand.

"Hey, Frankie, so good to see you!"

"Nice to see you, Claire." Frankie replied with a big grin.

Frankie was a rock in Claire's business. He wasn't highly ambitious nor was he wildly social, but he was dependable and even-tempered. He had a good spirit and truly desired the best for the people around him. Claire was deeply grateful for Frankie, and she hoped her interactions with him reflected that.

They all gathered behind the bar while Frankie passed out the copies Claire had asked him to make.

Written on the paper was a rough outline of the culture, values, and strategies that Claire had distilled and named in her work with Ronica.

As her three employees took a good look at the paper in front of them, Claire began. Violet listened attentively, and Frankie stood alert and at attention, ready to meet any of the café's needs should they arise during the meeting. Amber leaned against the counter casually, glancing away occasionally.

"So, as you guys know, I've been taking a workshop to learn how to make this place thrive, and I learned a lot," Claire told them. "Most importantly, I learned to be clear about what we are about here and how to focus on delivering that."

Violet nodded, looking from Claire back to the paper.

"I'll communicate more on that to you guys later, but for now, I basically just need to know if you guys are with me or not." Claire felt a little flutter of nerves in her chest and reminded herself of Ronica's injunction to be vulnerable. "And I hope you guys are with me because I really believe we can make this work and turn this place around if we do it together." Claire straightened up and brightened. "I think in a year, people won't even recognize this place."

She stepped out from behind the counter and took a good look at the coffee shop. "My vision is to host open mic nights here, and to make this a place where people love to come to, to get to know the community and to hear the talented artists that we have in this area."

She turned back around to her crew whose eyes were on her as she began to get more and more excited. "I'm talking comedians, musicians, poets, anyone and everyone. And I want that same culture to continue during the day, where people feel safe and comfortable here. Where people feel accepted."

Violet was nodding enthusiastically, her expression growing more animated. "Wow, I love that, Claire!"

Continuing to watch Claire, Amber dug some gum out of her purse, unwrapped it, and popped it in her mouth.

Frankie looked pensive as he scanned the room.

Claire continued, "But in order for us to do that, we have to embody that culture. We have to treat our customers like each one is the guest of honor. I want us to work this room and take care of people. Cater to their needs. Go above and beyond when they ask us questions. We can talk about this more later, but I'd go as far as to say that I'm okay with certain things not getting done if it means you get to spend more time spending time with our guests. Specifically, the ones who haven't yet felt welcome."

Frankie was nodding slowly, still thinking and processing.

Claire was on a roll. "And between us, we need a culture of consideration. Where each other's needs come before our own. Like where we really look out for each other. How are guests going to feel comfortable here if we're not accepting of one another and treating each other with the utmost consideration? That means we deal with conflict with respect. It means that it becomes weird to not want to help each other out, to only look out for yourself. We make a culture where we share the responsibilities. And honestly, a place where the people who don't want to help each other, feel uncomfortable."

Amber looked up from whatever she was tracing on the counter with her finger. "What do you mean?"

"I mean that if you're in a culture where everyone helps each other out and is picking up shifts for each other, and helping with cleaning duties, and looking out for one another, and you're always the one constantly helped but never helping, you're going to feel uncomfortable eventually."

"I guess I'm still confused," Amber replied.

"We're not about being perfect, making the best coffee in the city, or having everything together. We're about being comfortable and accepting others. Everyone from our classy young professionals to our misfit college students should feel welcome here." Claire looked back out toward the room, joy flooding through her as she envisioned the future.

Frankie cleared his throat. "Okay, so how do we do this?"

Claire looked back at him and smiled. "We'll get to that. But for now, are you guys with me or not?"

"Absolutely!" Violet, clearly excited, could hardly contain herself.

Claire wanted to run up to Violet and squeeze her, but she just beamed at her and said, "Excellent."

Frankie said, "Yeah, I'm in. Just tell me what to do."

"Great," Claire said.

Amber paused and looked at her colleagues and then back at Claire as they waited for her to respond. "Are you forcing us to be fake and peppy to people?" she finally asked.

Claire was taken aback. "No, not at all, Amber. Fake is the last thing I want. If you don't think that you can be genuine and be behind this mission, that's okay. But then this probably isn't the place for you to work."

Amber went on the defensive. "Well, I wish you would have told me that it was going to be like this before I started working here."

Claire relaxed. "I know. I'm sorry, Amber. I'm embarrassed to say that I didn't know what I was doing then."

Amber didn't move and stared at Claire, thinking as she chewed her gum. "Well, I'll try it."

Claire's expression grew serious. "Amber, you're a valued team member," she said gently. "Somehow, you make the perfect latte every time. But you're either in or you're out. We can't build a reputation on being empathetic and welcoming if our staff isn't consistent."

She could tell Amber was confused. She tried again.

"What I'm saying is that every time you come to work, your priority is to make every single person who follows you feel accepted, welcome, and genuinely cared for. That means looking out for peoples' needs even if it's unnecessary. That means if people want to be social and you have a moment, then be social." Claire paused for effect. "With *everyone*, not just your college friends."

Amber stared defiantly at Claire. Finally, she said, "I'm sorry, Claire, but that sounds exhausting. I just want to make coffee."

"I understand," said Claire. "Then I don't think this job is a good fit for you."

***

Claire had hurriedly scheduled an interview with Zoey, a friend of Violet's, for a couple of days later. Violet had recommended her enthusiastically as a candidate who would align well with Claire's new mission for her coffee shop.

Claire walked into the back office with Zoey, brushing her hair behind her ears and sitting down with a notepad and pen.

"I appreciate you coming in on such short notice, Zoey. I'm Claire Wallace, and I'm the owner of The Haunt. Like I said on the phone, we're making some changes around here, so we're trying to make sure our employees fit our mission."

Zoey, perky and upbeat, sat upright in her chair and nodded enthusiastically.

"Okay, Zoey, first question: How would your mother describe you?"

Zoey was caught off guard, but she answered gamely. "My mom would say that I'm stubborn in that I do whatever attracts me. Like studying literature even though it won't provide me with a stable job." She rolled her eyes a little and smiled. "Most likely. She would say that people don't intimidate me, big or small, and that I somehow seem to find the weirdest people to have a conversation with."

They both chuckled. Claire already loved this girl. But would she be a good employee? She handed Zoey a piece of paper.

"I'm going to have you fill this out. It's only a couple questions, and then we'll talk about it after."

"Sounds good," Zoey said, taking it.

They sat together in the silence, Claire jotting some notes as Zoey filled out the questionnaire.

"All right, I'm done." Zoey passed the paper back to Claire.

"Great." Claire looked it over quickly.

"All right, I'm going to ask you why you didn't pick the number below or above the number you picked. So, for 'Radical Hospitality,' you picked a six. Why not a five and why not a seven?"

Zoey thought for a moment. "I didn't choose a five because that seemed pretty low. I do love the idea of being hospitable, but I didn't choose a seven because I guess I'm confused on what radical hospitality even is. Like, do I bake snickerdoodle cookies for everyone to try out?

No. But do I believe that everyone deserves to be heard and served well? Yes."

Claire nodded and wrote down some notes. "Okay, on 'Sociable and Loving,' you put an eight. Why not a nine and why not a seven?" she asked.

"I didn't put a seven because it was too low," Zoey replied. "I really love being sociable, and I believe that comes from a loving place." She paused. "And I didn't put a nine because that seems like a superhero social person, who thrives mostly on social interaction, and I like my books too." She shrugged.

Claire had no doubt that she was telling the truth. "Okay, on 'Consideration,' you put a seven. Why not a six and why not an eight?" she said, looking down at the questionnaire then back up at Zoey.

"I guess an eight on consideration seems like someone whose focus in life is to be considerate, and a six doesn't seem considerate enough. I'm someone who is consistently considerate and caring and I hardly miss a beat, but I don't know if that's my focus in life."

Claire nodded, pleased with her honesty. She put down her pen and clasped her hands together on the desk. "All right, so let me share with you a little bit of what we are doing here. Ultimately, we want The Haunt to be an open mic-night place. So there will be evening shifts for you, and during those shifts, you'll be busy working the room and making sure everyone is well taken care of. Everyone has to feel comfortable and welcome, which is why I asked you those questions. Those questions reflect our values as a business. Those are the most important behaviors here.

"The reason we exist is to create a place where people feel accepted and connected, hence the open mic nights. You're expected to go above and beyond in how you interact with customers as far as making them feel welcome. No one should have to hunt for things like straws or napkins. People should have ready access to water, and you should be willing to explain everything to them on the menu at a moment's notice. If you're not busy, we encourage you to get to know our customers. No one should be treated differently from another person. Even if they are…unconventional.

"As far as working with the team, we value consideration. We should all feel that everyone else has our back even if that means doing some extra work because it will come back around to you as well. Our customers will feel this atmosphere themselves and see that we care deeply for one another. It will help create this comfortable place I'm talking about." Claire let out a deep breath. "How does that sound?"

Zoey was glowing with excitement. "It sounds amazing."

Claire smiled. "Great, then the last step for me is to check your references. I'll be in touch shortly."

"Thank you," Zoey said as she stood up and shook Claire's hand. She grabbed her coat and headed out, leaving Claire alone in her office.

Zoey was definitely promising, and Claire was relieved. She needed at least three people on her team to make this work. But Zoey's addition to the team would mean nothing if they weren't all on the same page.

Chapter 11: Customer Service

Claire and Griffin sat next to each other at the Hungry Falcon during the afternoon lull, drinking their seasonal pilsner and reading Ronica's newest post on the Coffee Shop Management Facebook page.

This one was about customer service.

Ronica had given several examples of customer service models and how some of them focused on being super friendly while others wanted to be professional. Some of them encouraged their employees to sit down with customers while others emphasized expertise.

What is your customer service goal? How are you going to reflect that with your style, and what authority will you give your employees to attain this? Make sure it is in line with your target customer.

They both leaned back into the restaurant booth and crossed their arms. Claire looked over at Griffin and laughed, realizing that they had done the same thing. Griffin quickly sat back up and grabbed his beer. "Cheers to customer service."

Claire picked up her beer and clinked it with his, "Cheers!"

They took a swig, and Griffin began. "Okay…what am I trying to accomplish with my customer service?" He frowned at the notes in front of him from the workshop.

"Aren't you trying to be fun, Griffin?" Claire prompted.

"I *am* fun," Griffin insisted in a very serious voice.

Claire laughed. "Yes, of course."

Griffin joined in the laughter. "You're right. I want to be casual and never stressed. We're serving businesspeople, so I want us to be so calm and chill that people feel weird being stressed there." Griffin narrowed his eyes as he continued. "I don't want our customer service to be about remaking people's drink a hundred times, though, and I don't want to cater to really fussy people who want their coffee heated to exactly 140 degrees." Griffin began typing on his laptop. "I'm going to measure our customer service by how chill our employees are during the hectic periods," he said, only half-joking.

Claire nodded, chewing on her pen absently.

"I do want my employees to go above and beyond in customer service," Claire said. "Whatever the customer wants, we do everything we can to make sure they feel known and loved in that moment. Like we'd jump through a million hoops to get them their perfect coffee."

Griffin looked at her like she was crazy.

"What?" she exclaimed. "It makes sense with my 'why'—'to create a space where people feel accepted and connected.'"

He nodded. "All right, all right. I'm sending all the crazies to you, then."

She smiled. "That's what we want."

"Okay, so what authority are you going to give your employees to do that?" Griffin asked.

A crazy thought rolled through Claire's mind. "Anything."

"What?" Griffin looked taken aback.

"*Anything*," she repeated. "They can do anything. Make the drink a hundred times over! If someone asks for chocolate shavings on their latte, then we'll shave chocolate for them. If someone wants jelly on their croissant, we'll find jelly."

Griffin's eyebrow raised. "And how exactly are you going to make this happen?"

"I'm not sure," Claire said, relaxing in her seat. "But the idea is that our employees have the permission to go above and beyond for our customers to make them feel loved and at home. Maybe I'll put aside some money for each shift that the employees can take from."

Griffin pointed at the screen. "Well, look at that, Claire. You're already way ahead."

Ronica's next message read: *Make it unexpected. Make your customer service a talking point. Zappos decided that they needed the best customer service to put them ahead of other online shoe retailers. The longest customer service conversation recorded at Zappos is ten hours long.*

Claire whistled under her breath. Just then, they were interrupted by a low, muffled vibration. Griffin grabbed his phone from his back pocket and stood up.

"Hello?" he said as he turned away from Claire.

Claire continued reading what Ronica had written in the Facebook group.

"What, are you serious? Do you need me to come over there?" Griffin's voice was alarmed.

Claire looked toward him apprehensively, trying to catch his expression, but his back was turned toward her.

"All right, all right. I'm glad they're okay. I'll swing by tonight. Okay, love you too. Bye." He hung up the phone and turned back toward Claire, taking a seat.

"Are you all right?"

He rubbed his hands over his face while Claire patted him on the shoulder. "Yeah, I'm good." He looked up at her. "That was my sister. Someone tried to break into my parents' home in the broad daylight, but they ran off when they saw Rooney. That's their Great Dane."

"Wow, that's awful, Griffin. I'm so sorry."

"Desperate people take desperate measures." He sighed and turned back toward the laptop. "I need to get them out of there."

Claire nodded in support. "You will."

"Anyway, let's keep going with this." He put his finger on the mousepad and scrolled down to read the rest of Ronica's message.

Have a measurement system that rewards the kind of service you want to see. People will perform on whatever they're being measured on. For instance, if Zappos measured their customer service by how many phone calls they were picking up, they could never meet their customer service goal of going above and beyond for each customer.

Claire nodded. "That part makes sense."

The message continued:

Make sure you have a great feedback loop. You and your customer are partnering to ensure you're providing great service. Make sure they know you actually care and make it easy and accessible for them. If you come to La Valeur, you'll see my picture with my personal number on each table, asking for feedback.

Griffin and Claire exchanged glances.

"I hate asking people to fill out a survey." Griffin grimaced.

"Well, there must be another more casual way, something that fits you," Claire said.

"Yeah, you're right. Hmmm. Why don't I just go around and chat it up with the customers?"

"Just don't be one of those people that's like, 'How is everything today, folks?'" Claire laughed. "I'm never honest with those people unless it's terrible."

Griffin chuckled. "Yeah, you're so right. I can be real." He grabbed the collar of his jacket and popped it up, imitating the hipster he already was.

Claire finished reading the message out loud.

You must have a good customer service system to recover from a customer service failure. You will make mistakes; customers know that. But they want to see how you handle it. You could gain a loyal customer depending on how you handle mistakes. Think LATTE:

L: Listen to them. Even if you already know the problem, people just want to be heard. Take the time to thoroughly listen to them.

A: Acknowledge the issue. Show that you understand that the problem is a pain for them.

T: Thank them. They're probably feeling pretty negative right now, so make them feel more positive by thanking them for addressing the issue.

T: Take action and make the solution 3x better than the problem.

E: Explain what you did.

"So, Griffin, if you're not going to make someone's drink a hundred times for them until it's perfect, how will you address mistakes?" Claire asked.

"Well, mistakes are different. Obviously, if we messed it up, we'll make up for it. Heck, I'll throw in a croissant if they want one. I'll be like, 'Here you go bud. Croissant on the house.'" Griffin pretended to place a croissant down on the table.

"I like that, actually. It's better than asking if they want a croissant. I always feel awkward when people ask me if I want something when I point out a mistake," Claire mused.

"Yeah, that's true."

"Well, because it fits my model, I'm going to top that, and I'm going to give them a gift card, a croissant, *and* another drink." She smiled proudly.

"Wow, you're really going for it." Griffin picked up his drink and held it in the air as he turned toward Claire. "To customer service that fits our culture and our target customers!"

Chapter 12: Inventory

It was first thing in the morning at The Haunt. The rain was beating on the windows while young men and women flowed into the cozy space, shaking the water off of their raincoats.

Claire was behind the cash register, welcoming all of her faithful customers.

Violet was next to her working on some fragrant chai-themed drinks, and Frankie was somewhere in the back working on paperwork.

A young woman in a grey beanie and khaki trench coat approached Claire.

"Hello! Welcome!" Claire greeted her cheerfully.

"Hello. One pumpkin oat latte please," the woman said.

After an audible, "*Oooh!*" from Violet, Claire turned to see her grimacing.

"What's wrong, Violet?" Claire asked.

"We're out of pumpkin…and oat milk," Violet admitted.

Claire turned back toward the woman and saw her disappointed expression.

"I really, really love your pumpkin oat lattes, and I was so looking forward to it," the woman said.

"I'm so sorry." Claire looked down, defeated. "How about a drink and pastry on us?"

The woman seemed to be okay with that but still not excited.

The next morning, Claire was back at the register when the same woman walked through the door.

Another "*Oooh!*" from Violet.

Claire's heart sank. "What, Violet? What could possibly be wrong?" she asked, but she already knew what it was.

Please don't ask for a pumpkin oat latte, please don't ask, she thought to herself as she turned back to the woman with a big smile.

"Hello, one pumpkin oat latte, please," the woman said.

Claire woke up with a start, her heart still pounding.

Coffee dreams were the worst.

She must have dozed off after pressing play on one of Ronica's videos. She refocused on the video playing in front of her as Ronica talked about inventory.

"Take a look at the products you're selling," Ronica was saying. "Do you sell a lot of products that go bad quickly?"

Claire rubbed her eyes and restarted the video, sitting straight up in her office chair and taking a sip of some lukewarm coffee.

"Inventory is more closely related to customer service than anything else," Ronica began. "If you run out of what people are looking for, that's just bad customer service. People value consistency. Most people, with few exceptions, value consistency over quality. If you make it like I had it last time, then I'm pleased. Inventory management is making sure you're managing in a way that doesn't compromise freshness nor availability."

Ronica shifted the camera toward a whiteboard she had filled with bullet points.

Order based on:

- *How long it stays fresh*
- *How much you use in a day (most and least)*
- *How long the item takes to reach you after you place a delivery*
- *Include a slight margin of error*

Try to make your inventory visual:

- *Paint the back of the shelf so you can see it when your stock gets low enough that you need to reorder*
- *Label each shelf so you know exactly where everything goes*
- *Make sure the newest items go to the back of the shelf*

"For example," Ronica said, "you paint the back of the shelf red. Now when you see the red, you know that there's six cartons of almond milk left. You use two per day, it takes two days for the shipment to be delivered, and you always have one day's supply for backup. When you see the red, you place an order."

Claire began scribbling down some notes.

Ronica was back at the spot Claire had woken up at. "Take a look at the products you're selling. Do you sell a lot of products that go bad quickly? The more volatile the products you sell, the more challenging it will be for you. Some baked goods go bad within hours. If you do have some of these products that are hard to keep in stock and go bad quickly, let the customer know that.

"For example, next to your freshly baked croissants have a sign that says, 'Baked daily and in stock until sold out.'" Ronica smiled at the camera. "That's it, everyone. Have fun and be sure to let us know how it goes."

The video stopped.

And just in case her terrible dream was some kind of crazy premonition, Claire wrote down in all caps, *PUMPKIN OAT*.

Chapter 13: Decision Making

Claire had never explored this side of the city limits before. Even though the landscape was becoming less urban, it felt rougher than what she was used to. Griffin was at the wheel of his dark green Subaru, and they were listening to Ronica's short clip about systematizing decisions. Griffin wanted to check on his parents since the recent attempted theft, and Claire had asked if she could go with him.

Street signs and dilapidated houses began to appear on the side of the road, and Griffin became noticeably more tense.

"Welcome to paradise," he muttered.

Broken down cars in people's yards, waiting for an unlikely future fix, seemed to be a common theme. A woman in a navy-blue tank top sat on her steps smoking a cigarette as she watched her kids run around the front yard.

"This is it." Griffin pulled into a driveway.

His parents' home was modest but well-manicured compared to the other houses on the street. Steps led to a porch, and the screen door was closed, but the front door was open behind it.

As Claire got out of the car, she could hear music playing, but she couldn't make out what kind. She was straining to hear it when it was interrupted by a deep bellow of a bark. Around the corner came a huge, tawny dog with dark jowls and pointed ears.

"Rooney!" Griffin shouted. "Get over here!"

The giant animal's demeanor changed immediately. It put its ears down and ambled over to Claire to sniff her out.

Claire stood erect and put out her hand tentatively. "Hey, Rooney," she said in the kindest voice she could muster.

"Rooney!" Griffin shouted again.

The dog gave Claire a quick sniff then quickly diverted direction toward Griffin, flopping his enormous body against Griffin's side for a good pet.

"Good boy." Griffin patted the dog's side.

"Well, you must rest a little easier, knowing that giant is here with your parents," Claire laughed, staring at the dog.

"Griffin, honey!" a voice called from inside, and Claire saw the figure of a woman appear in the door.

The door swung open, and Griffin's mom stepped out onto the porch. Her smile was so sweet that Claire warmed to her immediately.

"Oh hello, you must be Claire," she said kindly as she made her way down the stairs.

Claire held out her hand. "Yes, ma'am. So nice to meet you, Mrs. Robertson."

Griffin's mom ignored Claire's hand and pulled her into an affectionate hug. "So nice to meet you, Claire. You can call me Laura," she said as she pulled away.

Claire was oddly touched. She wasn't used to this kind of unstinting affection.

Laura walked over to Griffin and gave him the tenderest hug as if she hadn't seen him in years. Claire suddenly remembered that Laura had missed out on thirteen years of her son's life, even if he had been home for a year now.

"So good to see you, honey," she said as she pulled back but held onto his arms as she studied his face. "Come inside, dear."

Claire and Griffin followed Laura into her home, Rooney lumbering in after them.

"Please sit down, and I'll grab you two some tea." Laura made her way into the kitchen.

Claire meandered through the living room, past all of Griffin's old baseball pictures and family photos from decades prior. She sat down on the loveseat and immediately noticed the picture sitting on the end table. It was of a teenage Griffin and his parents at the airport, and they were holding him tight.

She picked up the photo and her heart swelled with emotions. Especially when she saw how proud his father looked.

Laura came back with a platter of mugs filled with hot water.

"Mom, I hate to bring this up, but I really wanted to check in on you," Griffin said. "Are you okay after what happened a couple days ago?"

Laura took a seat and opened a tea bag. Claire followed suit.

"I'm okay, honey," Laura said. "It was a little frightening because your father was at work. But I'm glad to have Rooney here." She dipped her tea bag into the hot water.

"Did you see them?" Griffin asked.

"Yes, I saw a man at the back door very briefly, and he was making some noise, but before I could make sense of it, Rooney came around the corner barking up a storm, and the man took off over the fence." Laura leaned over the arm of her chair and stroked the top of Rooney's head who was faithfully sitting next to her. "Maybe they thought no one was home."

"Oh, man, Mom, I really want to get you guys out of here." Griffin frowned, clearly frustrated.

"Oh, it's okay, honey, don't worry about us," Laura said, removing the tea bag from her tea. But Griffin didn't look comforted.

"Where's your husband today, Laura? Is he at work?" Claire asked.

"Oh yes, nine to five on the weekdays. He works as a janitor for the middle school."

"One day, I'm going to take care of you guys so Dad can retire." Griffin was obviously bothered.

"Griffin, honey, you don't have to carry our weight on your shoulders." Laura put her hand on her son's knee, looking into his eyes. "We're going to be okay."

Griffin rested his hand on hers and smiled at her, becoming playful again. "Okay, Mom, whatever you say. I get it, you're a superhero, nothing bothers you."

She chuckled and took a sip of her tea, smiling at Claire. "I'm just glad to have him back." Laura turned her eyes back toward her son. "It's so nice to have you home, honey. I know it wasn't easy coming back here."

Griffin nodded and leaned back into his chair. "It's nice to be close to you and Dad again."

"And for a long time, I hope, with your new coffee shop in the city." Laura beamed at him with pride and enthusiasm.

Griffin glanced at Claire and let out a deep breath. "Yup, that's the plan."

"Griffin's very fortunate to have you as a mother," Claire said. "I could only hope to have parents as encouraging and kind as you."

"Are you…not close to your parents?" Laura asked delicately.

"Well, they have their moments." Claire smiled a little. "I know that they love me, but let's just say my home was a couple degrees colder than this one."

"They must be dealing with some kind of fear," Laura said perceptively.

"Yeah, you might be right," Claire answered. "I find it hard to be honest with them because I'm afraid they'll be disappointed with me. I both desperately want to make them proud, but at the same time, I don't look forward to speaking to them."

"Have you ever tried being honest with them?" Laura asked. "What do they say?"

"Hmmm." Claire thought. "I haven't tried to be truly honest with them in a long time. I guess I've always felt they'll never change, so what's the point?"

"Maybe you should give them another chance," Laura said with compassion while Claire stared into her tea.

Then she looked up and caught Laura's warm gaze. "Yeah. Maybe I will."

***

Claire picked up her phone and stared at the entry that read "Dad."

What a thought, to be truly honest with her father. Would that just be releasing the floodgates of disappointment?

Or maybe it would be healing for both of them. How would she go about it in a way that didn't make him feel defensive? Maybe she could just try being open with him.

Claire dialed the number, her heart racing as the phone rang.

He didn't pick up. Voicemail. Maybe this was good.

"Hey, Dad, it's Claire. I, uh, I just spent some time with a good friend of mine and his parents, and I was thinking about you." She stopped. She couldn't do it. "And uh—yeah, I just wanted to let you know we're making progress. Your money is in safe hands."

She hung up and let out a frustrated sigh. Maybe someday, but not today.

***

Claire was in her office the next day when Violet knocked on the door.

"Hey, Violet, come in." Claire swirled around in her chair to face her.

Violet took a seat. "I was wondering if you'd hired Zoey?"

"Oh, yeah, I just need to call her," said Claire. "Her references all checked out. That was a great suggestion, thank you, Violet."

Violet smiled happily. "Yay, that's great!"

"Was that it?" Claire asked.

"Oh no, actually there's something else." Violet took out a pamphlet from her back pocket and passed it to Claire. "I'm in an anti-trafficking club on campus, and we're doing a fundraiser right now. I was wondering if I could set up a table with some information about it in the corner of the café?"

Claire looked at the pamphlet and pondered it. She had just listened to Ronica talk about making decisions and how to systematize them. What had she said?

"Let me think about it," Claire said. "I'll let you know tomorrow."

Violet nodded. "Thank you, Claire." She walked out of the office back to the front.

Claire opened up the Coffee Shop Management Facebook page and scrolled to Ronica's talk about decision-making:

"Systematizing your decisions is basically impossible if you haven't gained clarity on your coffee shop. You have to understand your culture, strategy, tactics, and finances before making decisions. But once you have that information, making decisions should be almost effortless. Decisions

that would normally be tough will become low stress because you know what your decisions must align with.

*Is this aligned with my mission?
Does this help me get toward my vision?
Does this align with my values?
How does this affect my target customers?
How will it affect my ability to meet other priorities?
How does it affect my financial situation?"*

Claire thought about her why and her desire to make The Haunt a comfortable place where people felt accepted and loved. She thought about her values: considerate, social and loving, and radical hospitality. Her vision was to open up multiple coffee shops that all specialized in providing a comfortable place for people to be known.

Raising awareness on human trafficking was a noble pursuit, an incredibly important one, but it did not fit her priorities. She was going to have to tell Violet "no" on this one.

She breathed a sigh of relief. This truly might have been something that racked her with insecurity in the past. Something good that was hard to say no to, but also something that would have been one of a million ideas pulling her in one of a million different directions.

The last part of Ronica's message was about delegating decision making.

There are five levels of delegation:

1. *Your employee handles it and is free to do whatever they want*
2. *Your employee handles it however they want but reports back to you on what was done*
3. *Your employee tells you how they will handle the situation first and must get your approval*
4. *Your employee conducts research and presents you with three options and you decide*
5. *Your employee has no authority and only follows orders*

6. Most companies are not clear about who has the authority to make what decisions.

Claire thought about Frankie and wondered if she had empowered him enough. She definitely trusted him and his ability to make decisions. It was very possible that he could be helping her more if she clearly delegated power to him.

She began writing out an authority document, detailing who could make decisions on:

1. Spending money
2. Offering new products on the menu
3. Giving away free items
4. Hiring
5. Firing
6. Posting on social media
7. Posting potentially controversial items on social media

Before Frankie could make decisions for The Haunt, she was going to have to fill him in on what she had discovered. Really fill him in—specifically and completely. It was time to communicate culture.

Part IV
Communicating Culture

Chapter 14: Foundational Culture

Claire had just returned from her first in-person meeting with her Coffee Shop Management cohort since their last class with Ronica.

Ronica had decided that it was a good idea for them to touch base in person and to learn a few new concepts before continuing on. Claire had specifically planned to meet with her crew after the meeting because she knew Ronica would be teaching them about communicating their culture to their staff.

But it had gone a little differently than Claire had expected.

Ronica had spent a large portion of the time talking about different types of culture within a business. Foundational culture was the culture that any successful business needed to have, and it consisted of five elements: belonging, trust, purpose, clarity, and accountability.

Distinctive culture was the culture that everyone had taken the time to distill for themselves.

Finally, strategic culture was the culture that aligned with her coffee shop's unique strategies. It was based on whatever would make that coffee shop successful, depending on the market, etc. Which made it the only culture out of the three that was ever-changing.

Beginning with belonging in foundational culture, Ronica had explained that people deeply desire to feel as though they belong. People desire to be a part of a special group and to feel like they matter within that special group.

Claire thought about how this was probably the biggest factor in why she stayed in the corporate world for so long. The specific company she worked for had made her feel like she was part of an elite group. Everyone who worked there talked about the company with pride.

Claire entered The Haunt and was greeted by the familiar faces of Violet and Frankie.

"Hey, you two." Claire walked behind the bar and began making herself some tea as Violet and Frankie gathered together at a table, drinking decaf coffee and herbal tea.

They had just finished closing down the shop and the only task left was sweeping.

Claire sat down with her small crew and inquired about their shift. Once they'd filled her in, she took in a deep breath. "Okay, y'all, now to why I kept you here tonight. I wanted to address that there will be some fundamental elements to our culture here, and these five elements will be: belonging, trust, purpose, clarity, and accountability."

Violet nodded, wide-eyed and alert. Frankie was always waiting for the practical notes.

Claire asked bluntly, "So do you guys feel like you belong here?"

Violet looked confused. "What does that mean exactly?"

"Do you feel that you're a part of something special, and do you feel like you specifically matter here?" Claire clarified. "Like you're not just another number?"

Violet couldn't help but laugh. "No offense Claire, but it's hard to feel like just another number when there's only three of us right now."

Frankie broke into a smile, and Claire chuckled. "You got me there."

There was a pause as they thought about this point, and then Frankie spoke up. "Can I be frank, Claire?"

"Please."

"I feel like I belong here in the way that I'm helping keep something together that has been suffering for a long time."

Claire grimaced.

"I do believe in you, Claire," Frankie continued. "And I believe that one day, we'll have something truly substantial here to feel like we're a part of. The place with the best open mic nights, that's something to be proud to be a part of."

Claire nodded. "I completely understand." She locked eyes with Frankie. "And you have been so essential in keeping this place alive, so thank you, Frankie." He nodded pleasantly and she continued. "Well, then it seems that you two know that you matter here, but as to what you belong to, that seems a little more convoluted right now."

They both nodded in agreement.

"And that's entirely my fault." Claire thought about the second element—trust—and how Ronica had mentioned how vulnerability precedes trust and the first person to be vulnerable should be her.

"I haven't done a good job with being clear because I didn't even know myself." Claire looked down at the table and fiddled with her tea bag.

"And I'm sorry that you guys got caught in the middle of that." She looked around at her loyal teammates and then back down. "I was in full-on survival mode, and I could barely see my hand in front of my face."

She paused and looked back up at Violet and Frankie with the gleam of hope burning in her eyes. "But I'm not there anymore," she assured them. "Now is the time to be intentional, and I'm grateful that you two will be around for the second half because you'll will get to see this place come alive with both purpose and clarity."

Frankie smiled at Claire like he was proud of her and pleased with her determination. Until recently, the Claire he'd known had seemed defeated and desperate.

Claire continued, "I don't want to set unrealistic expectations however—there are always going to be some things that remain slightly unclear. But what does need to be clear is our purpose: to create a space where people feel accepted and connected. I will do whatever I can to make sure that's always clear."

Frankie and Violet nodded like soldiers accepting a mission.

"Anyway," Claire continued. "I want you two to know that I will create a safe place to talk about weaknesses and failures. Especially with all the changes that are happening, if we want to improve, we have to be able to be vulnerable with each other. We all have weaknesses, and we all make mistakes. I'm not afraid of that."

"I don't like speaking in front of people," Frankie blurted out.

Violet and Claire cracked a grin as Frankie continued, "I'm not going up to the microphone, Claire, don't make me do it."

Claire laughed. "No worries, Frankie," she said. "Good thing I'm a mic hog."

"I get really overwhelmed in the morning rushes," Violet threw in. "And I'm not sure how to fix that."

Claire shrugged her shoulders, continuing the vulnerability chain. "I make everything important, so nothing is important."

They all paused and smiled at one another, and then Claire continued, "But Frankie, you're one of the most level-headed people I know. And Violet, I don't think you have one unkind bone in your body." Claire became attentive. "Plus, we'll work on systems that make it easier for you to manage in the morning."

Violet blushed but then quickly became uneasy as something passed through her mind. "Claire, with what happened to Amber..." She looked slightly apprehensive. "How do I avoid that?"

"Oh, you don't have to worry about that, Violet," Claire assuaged her. "Unless there are certain behaviors that I repeatedly hold you accountable to and you decide repeatedly that you don't want to adhere to them. At that point, I'm sure you'll have decided yourself that you don't want to work here because it'll be annoying to keep being corrected about something that you don't want to change. Amber just didn't want to be a part of the culture we're trying to create here. That's also different than if say, there's a skill that you're having a hard time with and you want to excel but it's difficult. I don't mind that, but I do mind people deliberately refusing to uphold our values."

"Okay, that makes sense," Violet said. "Well, I like everything you've talked about when it comes to your vision for The Haunt."

"Great." Claire smiled. "Then I can imagine that you'll be here as long as you want to be."

Violet seemed comforted by this and sat back in her chair with a grin.

"Which reminds me, Frankie," Claire said, "I'll need your help keeping people accountable to how we behave and do things around here."

Frankie nodded. "Yes, it's the only way to keep this place healthy and focused."

Claire smiled. "Yes, focus. Something I could use more of. Plus, I think that when our team sees how wonderful it is for our customers when we uphold our values, that they'll hold themselves accountable."

Frankie and Violet nodded in agreement.

Claire looked straight at Frankie. "But accountability without relationship will only cause resentment. The only way people will stay accountable to us, is if we maintain genuine relationships with our people."

Mildly shocked by the wisdom that had sprung from Claire, Frankie thought about this. He began thinking about all the authority figures in his life who had tried to keep him in check without genuinely caring for him.

"All right you two, I think that's enough for today." Claire looked down at the floor. "And don't worry about the sweeping, I'll take care of it."

Chapter 15: Strategic Culture

Claire had spent a little time with Jennifer at the cohort rendezvous the day before, but it had been a moment too short. She had asked Jennifer if it would be all right if she visited her at Obsidian to talk about how she was dealing with everything.

Obsidian looked just like its name. When Claire walked in, she was impressed by how much dark granite filled the space and how cutting edge everything looked. Even the menu was obviously geared toward people who knew something about coffee and were searching for something specific, something new and wonderful.

The woman behind the counter was wearing a perfectly ironed white shirt and black pants. She immediately locked eyes on Claire and made herself ready and available.

"Hello, I'm here for Jennifer," Claire said. "My name's Claire, she should be expecting me."

"Absolutely." The woman walked into the back.

Jennifer came out immediately. With her hair back in a sleek ponytail and her hip glasses, she looked like a researcher on the brink of a discovery.

"Hi, Claire," Jennifer said with a keen smile. "Welcome to Obsidian. Have you been here before?"

Claire looked around. "No, I haven't. I'd heard of it, of course. Sounds like the place for serious coffee mavens."

Jennifer seemed pleased. "Yes, that's who we cater to. Let me give you a tour."

"I'd love that!"

"Oh, how rude of me—can I get you some coffee first?" Jennifer asked.

"Oh yes, I'd love to try something. What are you most proud of?" Claire asked.

Jennifer's face lit up as if no one could ask her a better question. "Renée, could you make her some of the 2019 Panama?"

Renée nodded and quickly went to work.

"We've been working with these farmers for some time, and normally, we have a hard time buying naturally processed coffee because of the defects," Jennifer explained. "But because of our recent investment in a color sorter, we've been able to make something very unique."

Renée finished the coffee and Claire took a sip. "Whoa." She didn't understand as much as Jennifer did about coffee, but she could tell there was something special about this one. "This is truly something else."

Jennifer's eyes glowed. "Come with me, let me show you around."

Claire followed Jennifer into the backroom, and she felt like she was entering the laboratory of a mad genius.

Jennifer had a whole roasting operation going in the back, and there were even machines that Claire didn't recognize.

"What is that?" Claire said, pointing toward a smaller machine next to the roaster.

"That's a color sorter. It sorts out the defects for me and makes my life a whole lot easier," Jennifer said.

"Wow." Claire looked around in amazement. The space looked as though someone had meticulously planned every aspect of it.

Jennifer began pointing at different machines in the production line. "Our conveyor allows you to convey coffee to the roaster and to the sorter without ever having your coffee stored in a bin. The conveyor also weighs while in continuous operation because it has scales built into the hopper and cyclone."

She turned toward Claire and continued in a professional tone, "We found that removing storage bins from the workflow allows for more space as well as better workflow efficiency."

Jennifer pointed toward the end of the production line. "We do have one bottleneck right here when it comes to sealing the bags. But it's an expensive machine that requires a technician, so maybe in the future."

Claire nodded as if she was understanding everything, but she had never really dealt with roasting in her life. "Jennifer, would you mind—I think especially from you it would be helpful—sharing your strategic culture?" Claire asked. "It's interesting that Ronica talked about your strategies becoming a kind of culture in themselves, and I feel like here it's the most apparent out of all the coffee shops I've been in."

"Hmmm." Jennifer stroked her chin for a second and looked around the roaster space. "Yes, absolutely. I'm glad you asked, it'll help me to think about it more. Let's go to my office."

Claire followed Jennifer into an office with black leather furniture and several dark green plants in the corner. The desk, of course, was clear. Claire wondered if this is what Jennifer's mind looked like—clear and organized.

Jennifer opened up her computer and began scrolling. "Strategic culture, strategic culture… Ahh, found it." She scanned the document in front of her and then looked up at Claire. "So, as you can see, innovation is one of our highest priorities here, and the culture needs to live and breathe that. That means, strategically, we've decided we're not afraid of taking risks and making decisions that might seem far out.

"We've also decided that it's not enough to be innovative. We must be *on the cutting edge*. So, in that regard, we must be willing to spend money to obtain excellent innovations. And yet, we believe it's important to be intentional in order to be excellent, so we always take a period of time before making decisions."

Jennifer laughed. "Personally, I tend to be very frugal in my personal finances. My phone is five years old and the screen is broken, but I don't care to replace it. If I was that tight with business purchases, we would never be successful at innovation."

Claire nodded and laughed.

"What's funny?" Jennifer inquired.

"How different we are from each other," Claire said. "I mean, for instance, you have to spend money to continue with your culture of cutting-edge innovation, but I would say that my strategic culture involves being frugal and keeping costs low so I can afford open mic nights."

Jennifer nodded. "Yes, I see that."

"And I'm okay with making impulsive decisions. Of course, they have to be lined up with my culture, but our decisions most likely will not carry as much weight as yours because our reputation isn't as dependent on it and we're not spending as much money. I do wish we *could* spend more money, but that's just not our strategy," she finished.

"Right, which is the difference between your unique culture and your strategic culture." Jennifer was scanning the document in front of her. "Your unique culture already exists within you and that doesn't change, but your strategic culture puts aside personal preferences in favor of what's going to make you successful." Jennifer closed her computer and looked at Claire. "Does your team understand your strategy?"

"Mmm…" Claire tilted her head thoughtfully. "Not as well as yours does."

Jennifer nodded. "I think it would help them a lot if they understood why you are making the decisions you are."

"Yeah, you're right." Claire took another sip of her amazing coffee. "On a personal note, Jennifer, how are you doing? You seemed pretty overwhelmed when you left Ronica's workshop."

Jennifer had her hands clasped together in front of her on her desk and she watched Claire from behind her thick glasses. It didn't seem like Jennifer was asked questions like this often.

"Yes, I was definitely overwhelmed," Jennifer answered and then she looked out the glass wall that peered into the roasting space. "All I wanted to do was focus on my inventions and projects, but I felt like a hamster on a wheel that didn't know how to move forward, and it was driving me crazy."

Claire knew something about being driven crazy. "And how is it now?"

Jennifer took in a deep breath and exhaled. "Better." Her shoulders relaxed. "Definitely better. It actually hasn't been as difficult as I thought it would be. Ronica has made the process straightforward and effective. I'm already feeling freer, and operations feel more effortless around here."

"I'm so glad, Jennifer. I so want you to succeed," Claire assured her. "Where else am I going to get my bougie coffee?"

Chapter 16: Team Communication

Six months later

Claire was sitting on a table in The Haunt with her feet on a chair and a clipboard in her lap. Violet was sitting on the floor, drinking her favorite, a dirty chai latte. Frankie, with a pencil behind his ear, sat adjacent to Claire with his legs crossed, looking at some notes in front of him.

Zoey was leaning against the bar, casually drinking a matcha latte and sporting her famous high ponytail.

And then there was their newest hire, Jasper, an earthy young man with dreads and a zeal for the uncommon. Claire was finally making enough money to get more people on staff, which meant that she was able to take days off and focus more on administration and supervising.

After six months of communicating her culture to her team and implementing her strategy consistently, The Haunt was finally doing better.

Claire no longer had nightmares about her finances, and though it wasn't always a smooth road, she felt confident in the direction they were heading and the systems they had in place.

It seemed like her team was becoming more confident every day, and everyone shared a general sense of hope about what they could accomplish together.

They had begun hosting open mic nights a few months prior. They had taken some time to gain traction, but Claire felt they were onto something at this point. She was finding more ways to make it cost-effective, and not only were more people showing up, but more people were getting in front of the mic. It was becoming a dream come true, and she celebrated every small victory.

More importantly, she felt healthier. No longer the hamster on the wheel, she was enjoying the momentum of moving forward. And the burden was so much lighter now that she was focused, her teammates were on the same page, and there were good systems in place.

It was the beginning of the day and they were having one of their glorious "Coffee People" meetings.

One of the last lessons that Ronica had presented was about "team communication." She asked everyone to make decisions on how their team would communicate.

Through Slack? Emails? Would it be one-way communication or collaborative communication? She reminded her students to remember that the way a team communicates should reinforce the "foundational culture" by making sure it promotes trust, clarity, belonging, accountability and purpose.

Herself being someone who'd had terrible communication with her parents growing up, Claire wanted to be sure that the communication at her café was healthy.

She knew that if she taught her team to treat guests with grace, they would treat each other with grace, so in their "Coffee People" meetings, they all discussed the different people who were showing up, especially regulars.

They would ask questions like: "What do these people need?" or "How can we help this individual and love them a little more?" Everyone knew this was not a place to gossip or to be critical about people. Their words would be flavored with compassion.

And naturally, that's how they began to show up for each other. The natural byproduct of grace was vulnerability, which created the coffee shop's "immune system."

People felt safe talking about their weaknesses or problems that were arising because they knew they would be met with kindness, which in turn created solutions and exponential growth for the coffee shop.

Radical hospitality, check. Sociable and loving, check. Consideration, check. It was truly coming to fruition.

They decided that communication would happen through a logbook that one of the employees would write in at the end of their shift to update the team on anything that needed to be communicated.

In addition, information such about protocols, systems, culture, values, vision, tactics, and so forth were all written in a book in the office that was easily accessible.

Claire and Frankie also made it a point to consistently bring up these elements in their meetings in order to keep everyone on track.

"Has anyone noticed this girl that comes in and always orders a zebra latte and sits in the corner next to the bookshelf?" Zoey asked.

"Oh, yeah—she has really colorful hair, right? And she has this cool style?" Violet replied.

"Yeah, that's her!" Zoey exclaimed. "She's awesome. I mentioned our open mic, and she seemed like she was into it, but then she got nervous about it."

"Hmmm." Claire pondered with a smile. "Seems like someone who could really benefit from performing. Let's encourage her and continue to make her feel seen and comfortable here."

Violet and Zoey were nodding enthusiastically.

"All right, y'all, let's talk about what we've seen in each other this week," Claire began. "I'll start."

She turned toward Frankie. "Frankie, you were so poised and generous with the angry customer on Sunday. I could tell you caught him off guard with how genuinely kind you were toward him after he had been so off-putting."

Frankie smiled humbly. "Thank you, Claire. He was just having a bad day."

After each one took turns praising the people in their team, they made space for anyone to talk about areas they felt like they were struggling in.

Sometimes people had something they needed support in and sometimes they didn't. This was one of those times where everyone was content.

Then they moved onto planning the next open mic night, which was the following weekend.

Claire had just met with the people from the workshop for the last time a couple days before and had invited all of them to attend.

She was not surprised to learn that Stephen had left the café business and was now traveling around Europe in search of the next business venture. If you followed him on social media, it seemed like he was having the time of his life. She was happy for him.

Jennifer was still innovating, and Claire often thought about Obsidian and all of its wonders.

Griffin seemed to be finding more and more freedom every day. Griffin was one of those people that Claire jumped for joy for every time he reached a milestone. She wanted so badly for him to achieve his goals and for his parents to move to a better neighborhood.

Claire and Griffin had remained close friends and would often visit each other's cafés, holding each other accountable to their goals.

She was actually planning to visit Cuppa tomorrow.

As the team was discussing the next open mic, Claire looked down at her phone after feeling the slight buzz of the table.

It was a text from her dad: "How's the business going?"

Claire resisted the urge to roll her eyes. It was a harmless question, except for the fact that he asked her all of the time without ever asking how she was doing herself. Every time, she told him that things were getting better and better, but she was sure he wouldn't believe her until he had the money in his hands.

Claire flipped her phone over and returned to her meeting. The team was cheerfully sharing ideas and assigning tasks to one another, and in that moment, Claire was suddenly overwhelmed with gratitude.

Her heart swelled with joy, and she sat in silence, glancing at each one of her tender, hardworking teammates.

"Claire, are you okay?" Frankie suddenly asked.

"Oh yeah, yeah. I'm more than okay," she replied.

Chapter 17: Marketing Alignment

Griffin was behind the bar of Cuppa, pouring espresso when he heard a familiar voice.

"Hey, son!"

Griffin whipped his head up in search of the voice and locked eyes with his dad who was approaching the bar with his mom.

Griffin ran out from behind the bar with his arms open wide. "Hey, Dad! Welcome to Cuppa!"

Griffin embraced his father and then moved onto his mother and gave her a big hug with a kiss on the cheek.

"How's it going, honey?" his mom asked.

"Going well," Griffin said. "I'm so glad you guys are here, what can I get for you?"

"Oh, just some black coffee," his dad said.

Griffin smiled. "Coming right up. Go ahead and grab a seat!" he shouted over his shoulder as he made his way back to the bar. He was back a moment later with two cups of coffee which he placed in front of his parents. They'd chosen a colorful, modern couch near the window.

"Griffin, this place looks incredible," his mom said with wonder.

"Yeah, this is really something," Griffin's father said.

They had both been to Griffin's coffee shop before, but it had been months, and since that time the café had changed dramatically. The first time they'd came into the shop, they were already a crying mess of pride when they saw that their son owned a business in the city. But now they were seeing something quite different. There was a buzz in the atmosphere, and people were streaming in and out of the doors.

More importantly, though, they seemed to be genuinely enjoying themselves.

This felt like *the* place.

"You like it?" Griffin said with a smile as he sat down adjacent from them in a chair. "Thanks, Ma."

"You really changed a lot, didn't you?" Griffin's dad asked. It was rare that his dad was able to make it down to the café.

"Yeah, yeah. We focused a lot more on what we were trying to do, and we made some changes in accordance with that." Griffin took a look around, smiling from ear to ear. "Oh, and we just finished rebranding," he added. "I'll be right back." Griffin hopped up and walked back toward the office to grab some things.

He came back in a hurry with some papers in his hand, a coffee bag, and a mug. He set the items down on the table in front of his parents, next to their coffee.

The last lesson that Ronica taught them was about "Marketing Alignment." Griffin had wanted his marketing to reflect his "why" and his values. In a burst of inspiration, he'd hired a hip marketing coordinator to match his style and begun dreaming up a new brand.

What he got was colorful packaging with big letters to reflect the more relaxed atmosphere.

The ads and products were centered around his idea of being a place of respite in the city. A place where businesspeople came to relax and take a break. A place where friends came to socialize and dream and get creative.

He remembered Ronica's words: "Most companies are afraid to let their marketing be aligned with what it is they're all about."

Griffin's marketing conveyed that Cuppa was a welcome oasis from the rat race of the city, and sure enough, when his parents looked around, they saw students who were dreamily working on art projects and businesspeople calmly drinking their coffee. Everyone seemed relaxed and calm.

One of the mugs said, "Pause. Reject the culture."

Griffin was brimming with excitement. "What do you guys think?"

His mom began crying.

"Oh, Mom, why do you always have to cry!" Griffin teased her, lightly pushing her shoulder.

"It's just so amazing to see you happy, honey, and fulfilled." She sniffed, looking for a tissue in her purse. "And this place is wonderful. People seem really happy here. I'm so proud of you."

His dad continued. "Yeah, it's really great, son. Even your employees look like they're having a good time."

Griffin looked back and laughed. "Yeah, I think they are."

Just then, Claire walked through the doors. When she saw Griffin's mom, Laura, her face lit up and she let out a very enthusiastic, "Hey, guys!"

Laura got up and gave Claire a hug, and then Claire turned her attention toward Griffin's dad. "Hi, I'm Claire, a friend of Griffin's."

Griffin's dad got up and shook her hand, "Nice to meet you Claire, I'm Michael."

"A pleasure to finally meet you, Michael, I've heard amazing things about you," Claire said genuinely.

Michael's cheeks turned red. "Oh, what kind of hogwash are they making up about me now?"

They all laughed, and Claire sat down to enjoy the afternoon with Griffin and his parents.

Chapter 18: The End

Griffin was growing out his beard again with the start of fall, which perfectly matched the aesthetic of his new hobby.

There was a soft thud as the axe landed almost directly in the bullseye.

"Nice!" Griffin said, a small cloud of breath leaving his mouth.

Axe-throwing: edgy and exciting, this was his kind of hobby.

He looked down at his watch. "Time to go," he muttered to himself, taking one last look at the bullseye with a satisfied smile.

Griffin turned around to look at the modest but charming home behind him. Tufts of smoke were escaping out of the chimney and a light glow was radiating from the windows on the backside of the house.

Griffin caught sight of his mom at the window above the kitchen sink. She looked up from her dishes and waved at him with her sweet smile.

It hadn't taken long for his parents to get used to their new home in suburbia, although at first, his mom said she felt like an alien, living amongst all the suburban people. But within a few weeks she was friends with most of her neighbors, and Griffin imagined that she was known as the "sweet old woman next door."

His dad was still working at the school in their old neighborhood, but retirement was just around the corner, and Griffin was excited for that day.

Griffin strode over to the back gate of his parent's yard that faced the woods and set the axes down by a tree stump on the way out. Just then, Rooney trotted over to Griffin, trying to make his escape with him.

"No, boy, you stay here." Griffin slid out through the gate. "Take care of them, okay?"

He jumped into his Jeep and took off back toward the city. Thirty minutes later he was pulling up to one of his new favorite spots, The Haunt.

Claire was just getting up to address the crowded room when Griffin walked through the door. He quickly took one of the last available seats, and a huge grin crossed her face as she began to speak. "Welcome, everyone, how are you guys doing tonight?"

Whistles and clapping filled the room, and Claire nodded her head enthusiastically. "All right, that's awesome."

She looked down at her notes. "Well, welcome to The Haunt's open mic night. My name is Claire Wallace, and I'm the owner of The Haunt and your host for the night."

Violet approached Griffin as he watched Claire with joy. "Hey, Griffin, welcome. Can I make you something?"

Claire continued, "I'm super excited for tonight because we have some great performers that I've really been wanting to hear, so on that note—"

"Yes, an affogato, please. Thank you, Violet," Griffin whispered.

"Please welcome to the stage, Miss Cora Gallagher!"

The room erupted with whooping and cheering as a young woman with colorful hair took the stage. A guitar was strapped across her chest.

Her smile was nervous, but her eyes were shining with excitement as she leaned in toward the mic. "Hello, everyone, my name is Cora Gallagher. I've been wanting to do this for a long time, but I never had the courage, and probably still don't, but here we are."

The room clapped and hollered in support. Zoey yelled from the back, "You got this, Cora!"

Cora smiled timidly and began strumming her guitar.

Claire was making her way to Griffin when a familiar figure caught the corner of her eye. Claire looked to the front door to see her dad in his trench coat and classic gentleman's hat.

She quickly moved through the crowd until she was right in front of her dad. "Hey, Dad," she said kindly. "Can I take your coat for you?"

"Oh, hello, Claire. Yes, that would be fine." He began shedding his trench coat. "Wow, there's quite a lot of people here."

She detected a hint of disapproval in his voice but pushed it away. "Yeah, it's open mic night." She cocked her head toward the back of the room. "How about you follow me into the office real quick?"

"All right." He looked dubiously at the crowd but pushed his way through after Claire, and into her office.

Claire sat at her desk and took something out of one of the drawers. She noticed her father looking around her office. His gaze landed on a picture of him with Claire and Claire's mom at Claire's college graduation.

She quickly scribbled something on a piece of paper then stood up and handed it to her dad with a smile on her face.

"What's this?" He looked down at the paper.

It was a check for the amount of money he had loaned Claire to start her business, and then some.

"Claire, are you sure you can afford to give me this?" he asked.

Claire could hear Cora singing a sweet melody out in the café and was sad that she was missing it. But what truly mattered was that Cora was out there doing it, and she was doing a great job.

Claire took a moment to make sure her words were flavored with grace, but her posture became intensely serious. "Dad, all I wanted was to make you proud." He looked taken aback by her frankness. He began to speak, but she cut him off. "After all of this, when are you going to start believing in me?"

He looked down at the check, uncomfortable. "I do believe in you, Claire, or I wouldn't have given you the money."

Claire lightly put her hand on his arm. "Then please, show me."

He looked at her graduation picture again and didn't say anything. Silence filled the room. For a moment, she thought he might say something, but instead, he reached for his trench coat and nodded at Claire, holding up the check. "Thank you, Claire."

"Thank you, Dad," she said. She wanted him to stay for the open mic, she wanted to say more, but it would all come in time.

She followed him out of the office and watched him push through the crowd again. But just as he was about to walk out of the front door, he stopped to watch Cora. For a moment, there was wonder on his face, and then he left into the cold of night.

Cora held a long, forlorn note with her voice as the audience held its breath, captivated. She strummed the guitar one last time then abruptly stood up and smiled. The room exploded in applause, shouting, and whistling. Cora's face was glowing with joy as she bowed and then jumped off the stage. Nothing would be able to remove that smile from her face for the rest of the night.

Claire congratulated Cora and gave her a hearty pat on the back as she was exiting the stage. "Wow, that was amazing, wasn't it, y'all?" Claire asked the crowd.

More whistling and whooping.

"All right, and now it's my pleasure to introduce to you our one and only Violet!"

Claire jumped off the stage to the sound of applause as Violet hopped up. An arm caught Claire as she was walking over to the bar and Claire whirled around to see the familiar eyes of Maggie.

Excitement poured from Maggie's eyes. "You did it, Claire."

Claire's heart swelled and she pulled Maggie into an embrace. "Thank you, Mags." Claire whispered in her ear.

Claire locked eyes with Maggie's new husband who was standing behind her and Claire pulled away from Maggie.

"Hi Johnny, welcome in." Claire beamed. "Thank you for coming tonight."

Johnny smiled brightly. "It's a pleasure to be here."

Claire suddenly noticed Ronica and Jennifer sitting in the corner together, drinking affogatos and watching the show.

From across the room, Claire caught the look in Ronica's eye as she smiled at Claire. Her look of pride stopped Claire dead in her tracks, and the sound of the room seemed to fade away.

It was in that moment, that Claire knew: She was well on her way to her dream coffee shop.

CPSIA information can be obtained
at www.ICGtesting.com
Printed in the USA
JSHW041150160322
23845JS00001B/1